DISCOVERING THE INNER SELF

The Complete Book of Numerology

Dr David A. Phillips

Published and distributed in the United States by: Hay House, Inc., P.O. Box 5100, Carlsbad, CA 92018-5100 • *Phone:* (760) 431-7695 or (800) 654-5126 • *Fax:* (760) 431-6948 or (800) 650-5115 • www.hayhouse.com • *Published and distributed in Australia by:* Hay House Australia Pty. Ltd., 18/36 Ralph St., Alexandria NSW 2015 • *Phone:* 612-9669-4299 • *Fax:* 612-9669-4144 • www.hayhouse.com.au • *Published and distributed in the United Kingdom by:* Hay House UK, Ltd. • Unit 62, Canalot Studios • 222 Kensal Rd., London W10 5BN • *Phone:* 44-20-8962-1230 • *Fax:* 44-20-8962-1239 • www.hayhouse.co.uk • *Published and distributed in the Republic of South Africa by:* Hay House SA (Pty), Ltd., P.O. Box 990, Witkoppen 2068 • *Phone/Fax:* 2711-7012233 • orders@psdprom.co.za • *Distributed in Canada by:* Raincoast • 9050 Shaughnessy St., Vancouver, B.C. V6P 6E5 • *Phone:* (604) 323-7100 • *Fax:* (604) 323-2600

• *Edited by:* Rachel Eldred • *Designed by:* Rhett Nacson

First edition published by Angus & Robertson in 1980,
with 12 printings up to 1990 Reprinted in 1992 by Pythagorean Press

Second edition published 1996, and reprinted 1997, 1998 and 2000

ISBN 1-875281-10-X

07 06 05 04   4 3 2 1
1st printing in Australia (3rd Edition), October 2004

Printed in Australia by Griffin Press

DISCOVERING THE INNER SELF

The Complete Book of Numerology

DR DAVID A. PHILLIPS

CONTENTS

Note for Australian and English readers: Dates appear month first, then day, followed by year. For example, 12/27/2002 is December 27, 2002.

FOREWORD

In our lives, we've all had individuals cross our paths who effect a profound influence on its direction. When I first met David, I knew absolutely nothing about publishing books. His insights and advice have benefited not only myself, but also the hundreds of authors I now publish.

This book has been through many metamorphoses, and I felt part of its evolution should be to bring it into the new millennium. And so, to honour his memory, our friendship and the extensive study he did into the Science of Numbers, *Discovering the Inner Self–The Complete Book of Numerology* was carefully edited to give it a contemporary feel.

David was a devoted father and a loving husband. The support and encouragement he got from his wife, Delwyn, and his family ensured that whatever his lifetime goals were, he scored straight between the posts.

– Leon Nacson

CHAPTER .01

Numerology – The science of self-discovery

My life radically changed when I met Hettie Templeton in 1954. Not quite sure of my career choice to be an electrical engineer, my friend Bill Christopher suggested I see Mrs T. and "have your numbers read."

Though my student days were devoted to the use of numbers, to comparing quantities and solving equations, I was yet to be convinced that numbers could be used to unravel life's problems. Yet within five minutes of meeting Mrs T. my doubt dissolved.

Equipped with only my birth date and my name, Mrs T. told me things about myself that I thought only I knew. That hour with her changed my life's direction. It gave me a confidence I had not previously known and explained many "mysterious" past events. I was fascinated. So the following year, coinciding with my postgraduate research into medical electronics, I commenced study in numerology, the Science of Numbers.

Over the many long years that I have studied numerology, I've learned that there is no better way for us to understand ourselves, or our personal connections with others.

So many people spend so much of their time zigzagging through life, bouncing from experience to experience as though caught in a pinball machine. We simply do not know our own minds, nor the appropriate path(s) to take. And though there are countless courses and seminars available today devoted to personal growth, the information overload often creates psychological and intellectual indigestion – and a whole new experience of inner confusion.

Numerology, on the other hand, provides direct knowledge of the inner self, and from this basis of self-understanding, we are able to direct a determined course through life.

Numerology recognises that numbers are vibrations, and each vibration is different to the next due to the number of cycles it oscillates at per second. The variation in each case is a number. Every sound, colour, fragrance and thought is a vibration, and each dances to the tune of its inherent number, each in its distinct way connected to life. Thus, it doesn't take too much imagination to realise that human life has an intimate connection with numbers, for they are the very essence of life's expression.

As such, understanding numbers provides us with a simple and accurate meaning of our life in the same way as a road map helps us to navigate a route we have not previously travelled.

Pythagoras reveals the wonder of numbers

Born in 608 B.C., Pythagoras sought to free the human mind from political and religious confinement. Pythagoras gathered about him an ever-increasing number of students keen to aspire toward personal independence, and to discover the meaning of love and life. The essence of his teachings was enshrined in the axiom: "Know thyself, then thou shalt know the universe and God."

Pythagoras founded his own university at Crotona, a Greek colony in southern Italy, around 532 B.C. Admission was open to all who sincerely sought to learn. There was no distinction between sex, race, colour or creed. However, every person who entered had to make a commitment to intense study.

The major course taught was in self-development, and was provided in a three-part curriculum. The primary component was known as "Preparation." It consisted of intensive training in the "ten mathematical disciplines," designed to provide the student with "empire over the self."

The second trimester was called "Purification." Its essence was the understanding of life, its purpose and how to work in harmony with that purpose, as taught through the "Science of Numbers," more commonly known today as numerology.

In the final trimester, students were taught the concept of "Perfection." Perfection embraced the integration of the physical, mental and spiritual components of each person and of life.

*This book is offered to the keen student of life who, perhaps unconsciously, has been searching for "Purification," for the answers to life's many unsolved enigmas, it is a complete course in numerology based on the original Pythagorean teachings. You will discover who you really are and how you can further improve and understand your life. Numerology can also help you to relate better with other people, become more emotionally and financially secure, maintain good health and live a thoroughly loving life.

CHAPTER .02

The inner self revealed

*W*ithin each person is a beautiful light waiting to shine forth, a magnificent being aching for expression. That is the inner self, our individuality, our essential uniqueness. But this is not what we generally present to the world. Instead we have produced a "personality," a composite expression at the crux of which is our individuality (our inner self).

The average person is often two people. That which is freely expressed is usually the image, while the real person, the unique individuality of our inner self, is all too frequently suppressed. The image is something of an emotional ghost we have cultivated to defend our sensitivities. But we sell ourselves far too short, for our image can never hold to the beauty and grandeur of our natural inner self.

The acute sensitivity of the inner self is often mistaken for vulnerability, and as a consequence we build up a psychological wall. We stifle it, refusing to give it air, exercise and expression.

We begin to understand the inner self only when we start to understand who we are, where we have come from, our purpose in choosing this life and how to achieve that purpose.

In varying ways, we are all searching, but generally the search is for something external. We need to realise that the answers lie within, for as thinking, sensitive people, we need more answers to life than religion, politics or science have so far delivered. We need guidance, not promises; examples, not theories. And this is what I hope to deliver in the pages that follow.

The Science of Numbers, as originally taught by Pythagoras, is about to be revealed. Are you prepared for an exciting journey... a journey that will take you to the heart of your inner self?

CHAPTER .03

A metaphysical understanding of numbers

To the material scientist, numbers are merely symbols of comparative quantity. To the metaphysical scientist, or numerologist, numbers assume a more profound significance. They represent aspects of what it is to be human. In numerology, all numbers develop from and are connected to the absolute number, 1, for this number represents the expression of the ego, without which human life is expressionless and would cease to exist.

To truly understand numerology we must first know the essential metaphysical meaning of the numbers as based on the original arcane meanings taught 2,500 years ago by Pythagoras.

○ **ONE** is the first physical number. As the only absolute number, it is the symbol of divine expression. It is the key to verbal self expression and the expression of the ego as a microcosm of the divine (the macrocosm). It is the key to our communication skills.

○ *TWO* is the first spiritual (feeling) number. It represents the duality of humans and symbolises the gateway to our sensitivities, as well as our need to be part of a pair. It is the number of intuition.

○ *THREE* is the first mind (thinking) number. Following the primary verbal (1) and intuitive (2) expressions comes the mental. It is the gateway to the conscious mind and to rational understanding, the focus of left-brain activity, the key to memory. The number 3 is symbolised by the triangle, representing the connection of mind, soul and body.

○ *FOUR* is the number at the centre of the physical (doing) plane, the key to orderliness, practicality and organising. It is symbolised by the square, the basis of all practical construction.

○ *FIVE* is the centre of the soul (feeling) plane and the very centre of the total Birth Chart. It is the spiritual number representing love and freedom of expression.

○ *SIX* is the centre of the mind (thinking) plane, where it represents creativity, the integration of the left and right lobes of the brain. It also represents the opposite of creativity – destruction. This is "negative" creativity expressed as worry, stress, anxiety and depression.

○ *SEVEN* is the symbol of the temple, the human body and its seven chakras or power centres. It is the teaching learning number, the number of practical philosophical experience. Such learning is usually acquired through sacrifice as the means of indelible instruction.

○ *EIGHT* is the most active spiritual number, situated at the active end of the soul plane. It is the number of wisdom expressed intuitively through loving action. It brings independence into focus.

○ *NINE* is the three-fold number at the action end of the mind plane. As mind in action, it represents ambition (the physical aspect), responsibility (the thinking aspect) and idealism (the spiritual aspect), and so combines the attributes of each of the previous numbers.

○ *ZERO* is a symbol rather than a number. The 0 is present in many birth dates and has an important symbolic significance. Philosophically and mathematically, it represents nothing (as the numerator) and everything (as the denominator), the two infinite ends of the finite, neither of which is physically attainable. Thus, it is a totally mystical symbol, indicative of the degree of spiritual mysticism inherent (but rarely developed) in the individual. Anyone who has one or more zeros in their birth date has an inherent spirituality that they should recognise, for it has the potential to assist them to understand many of the deeper aspects of life (such as life's purpose, the power of thought and the process of reincarnation).

CHAPTER .04

The three aspects of self

*T*o penetrate the deeper level of human awareness (which numerology allows us to do), it's important to understand the three-fold nature of human being, and how our "three selves" are intimately connected.

Three terms are used to succinctly and simply describe our three selves: Basic Self, Conscious Self and High Self. Let me explain each in turn.

○ *Basic Self*

The primary level of human expression is through the body. The initial cry of the newborn baby, the adult's yell for help, the last gasping word of the dying – they all emanate from and through Basic Self. It is at this level that the child attains practical familiarity with its environment. Expression of the five physical senses (seeing, hearing, touching, tasting and smelling) constitute the primary functions of Basic Self, together with talking, laughing, crying and all other physical activities.

Basic Self motivation is largely reactive once we have grown old enough to master the physical activities in our environment. It is the body in self-defence; it is instinctive behaviour (as distinct from the intuitive behaviour of High Self). Insecurity, sensation seeking, the desire for control of situations or of other people, or just blatant exhibitionism are the expressions of Basic Self. Basic Self people are ego-motivated and their wants (desires or demands) often supersede their needs (requirements and preferences). They are noticeably left-brain motivated.

An understanding of numerology will be of considerable help to such people, who will learn to contain Basic Self so that it is the slave of the ego not its master and so life's lessons are readily recognised without need for harsher repetition and compounded sacrifice.

Let us never forget that Basic Self is vital to balanced expression while in the physical body. In fact, it is the body in action when total integration with the other two "Selves" is present. Otherwise, it is the body in "reaction."

As we learn to control Basic Self, it becomes our faithful physical servant. Ego is then motivated by compassion and wisdom, our physical lives become organised and we become more patient with ourselves and others. Our lives become less sacrificial as we become more philosophic. We evolve from the victim to the victor.

Basic Self in its fullness is the positive connection of the three numbers of the Physical Plane: 1, 4 and 7. (See Chapters 5 and 6.)

○ Conscious Self

Conscious Self is the home of our thoughts and attitudes. It can also be the home of our joy and sadness as well as our ability to *choose* either joy or sadness. It is the domain of memory, creativity and idealism.

Conscious Self is the bridge between Basic Self and High Self, integrating our reactive and instinctive aspects with our spiritual values. It is the connection between the left and right lobes of our brain.

When it chooses to be negative, Conscious Self becomes "unconscious self." It becomes deceitful, reactive, evasive and stress-ridden, and adopts the role of the poorly-done-by victim.

However, if we allow it to fulfil its ultimate purpose, Conscious Self is the great appraiser. It translates spiritual awareness into physical consciousness. Conscious Self helps us to interpret intuition, love and wisdom. It's the place where knowledge, compassion and wisdom is translated into positive action.

Conscious Self is anchored in the memory; it links past knowledge with present experience to create a repository of pertinent information. When used positively, this repository becomes the basis of our confidence and self-esteem, and expands to embrace enhanced creativity and, even further, intelligent idealism.

The three numbers of the Mind Plane are 3, 6 and 9, and they unite to empower Conscious Self.

○ *High Self*

High Self includes our moral virtues, philosophical ideas and spiritual values. It is the essence of sensitivity and feeling, the aspect of our being that recognises and determines our needs. It expresses itself as intuition, love and wisdom. It is our highest form of expression, the God within. Action through High Self is largely right-brained: creative, spiritual and compassionate.

Many people confuse love with emotions. True love is a function of High Self. Physical attraction (Basic Self) and mental conditioning (Conscious Self) frequently accompany love, but not necessarily. Love has a depth that permeates every facet of positive human expression. It enjoys expression through the emotions, but it is not governed by the emotions.

High Self is best facilitated through the development of our intuition, which leads to a depth of personal freedom. Attendant to such freedom is a newfound wealth and compassion. It leads to a depth of wisdom that is almost legendary in human expression.

In numerology, High Self is represented as the Soul or Feeling Plane, comprising the numbers 2, 5 and 8. The new millennium (with every birth date at least including a two) will see a more genuine spirituality manifested in human affairs.

CHAPTER .05

The Birth Chart

*W*hen we want to open a locked door, we need the key. For most people, the inner self is behind a locked door, for rarely do they discover who they really are or develop their ultimate potential.

The key to discovering the inner self through numerology is the Birth Chart. The primary purpose of the Birth Chart is to reveal at a glace the overall formula or pattern of our strengths and weaknesses. Each different birth date results in a different Birth Chart – there are almost endless variations, but the construction is always the same.

Handed down from teacher to teacher over the centuries in its pure, uncorrupted from, let me introduce you to the noble simplicity of the Pythagorean Birth Chart.

STEP 1

Convert your birth date to its full numerical equivalent. For example, if you were born January 21, 1963, you would convert it to 1/21/1963. (Always remember to include the full year.)

STEP 2

The Birth Chart is constructed of four short, straight lines: two drawn horizontally, two vertically. The vertical lines intersect the horizontal lines like a noughts-and-crosses layout.

This empty Birth Chart is symbolic of a baby as yet unborn.

STEP 3

Each of the nine spaces is the permanent home for each of the nine numbers. Whenever a number appears in a birth date, it must always be placed in its own space, nowhere else. If numbers are absent from the birth date, the corresponding spaces of the Birth Chart remain empty.

If all numbers were present in the birth date, the completed Birth Chart would appear as fully balanced:

3	6	9
2	5	8
1	4	7

This reveals no missing numbers; it further reveals an impossibility. The most numbers we can have in our birth date is eight, of which the numbers 1, 2 or 3 must be repeated. The maximum number of spaces that can be filled in a Birth Chart is seven, such as when a person has a birth date of 5/27/1983.

3		9
2	5	8
1		7

How we handle the Birth Chart when any number in the birth date is repeated is exactly the same as the previous example. For example, take the birth dates 11/11/ 1999 and 2/20/2000. The two Birth Charts would appear as:

11/11/1999

		999
11111		

2/20/2000

222		

Obviously, the maximum number of empty spaces on a Birth Chart for the 20th century is seven, while for the 21st century it is eight.

A further important aspect is the absence of 0 from any Birth Chart. (Its value and purpose were explained in Chapter 3.) Its repeated presence in a birth date reduces the prevalence of Birth Chart numbers, and in turn reveals vital growth needs as in the second example. Though this person's spiritual powers are heightened, the Mind and Physical Planes are poorly undernourished.

To construct your own Birth Chart, simply draw a naked Birth Chart and fill in the spaces with your birth date numbers.

STEP 4

With your Birth Chart now constructed, you have your basic individuality formula in place. We are now ready to analyse its many and various aspects. But first we need to observe the overall Birth Chart in its entirety, as a key to unlocking vital secrets of the inner self.

We must recognise the three Selves as expressed on the three Planes that comprise the Birth Chart.

MIND PLANE (mental, thinking)	3	6	9	CONSCIOUS SELF
SOUL PLANE (spiritual, feeling)	2	5	8	HIGH SELF
BASIC SELF (practical, doing)	1	4	7	PHYSICAL PLANE

Here we see the balanced Birth Chart with its three Planes and their meanings. The degree of concentration of numbers on each Plane gives a general indication of which Self is most fluently expressed.

This knowledge is extremely beneficial in human relationships, for it reveals the level of communication most favoured by each person. How much better would be our rapport with our spouse, children and work colleagues if we instantly knew their preferred Plane of expression, ie. with which Self they most identified.

The following example clearly illustrates this important aspect of numerology:

Shirley Maclaine, born 4/24/1934

3		9
2		
1	444	

In spite of her 1980's lapse into New Age spirituality, Shirley's Birth Chart formula clearly reveals her Spiritual Plane to be her weakest. Her dominant strength appears in her Physical Plane with her compounded 4s. Little wonder she was so easily enticed back to work in the entertainment industry. This is not to say that she has deserted the spiritual, for it is clear that she needs to develop this undernourished aspect of herself. But is she prepared to give it as much focus as it needs, or is she content with being the "New Age guru" she speedily became when, in fact, she was but a novice in the field!

The Meaning of each plane

Mind Plane

The Mind Plane represents the human head, and is symbolically found on the top line of the Birth Chart. It embraces memory, thinking, analysing, rationalising, imagining, creating, responsibility, ambition and idealism.

Soul Plane

The Soul Plane represents the human heart, and is symbolically found in the centre of the Birth Chart, from where it governs sensitivity. It also embraces intuition, love, freedom, positive emotions, artistic expression, spiritual independence and wisdom.

Physical Plane

The Physical Plane represents human activity, and is symbolically found at the base of the Birth Chart. It embraces verbal expression, motivation, body language, organisation, patience, materialism and learning through sacrifice.

○ *The numbers on your Birth Chart*

○ NUMBER 1

Located at the entrance to the Physical Plane, the number 1 refers to the expression of the physical body in terms of its relationship to the outside world. It is usually a reliable indication of the extent to which a person reacts to other people and circumstances (the immediate environment). It tends to indicate the degree of personal self-control – or its lack. This number is the foundation of the personality, for it represents the ego and how it is expressed or suppressed.

○ ONE 1

Birth dates with a single 1 belong to people who have some difficulty in verbal self-expression. This is not to imply they cannot speak well, rather it indicates the difficulty they have to give clear explanations of their inner feelings.

They can be forceful orators when the subject doesn't involve the expression of personal feelings, but fall short of putting into words their attitudes or conduct. Until they develop adequate self-mastery – a product of maturity and understanding – self-expression will not come easily to them.

At times, they will intentionally say the opposite of what they mean as a form of aggressive defence, intended to hurt or offend as a self-protection mechanism. This invariably compounds the initial problem, leading to some frightful arguments. They must learn to think before they speaking, and can do so by taking conscious command of their responses rather than reacting in the moment, as the spoken word is often impossible to retract and hurt feelings are difficult to mend.

To overcome this limitation take a blank notebook. Head the first page with today's date. Then tonight before bed take a few minutes to write down your thoughts and feelings about the day. Be sure to cover the things you didn't do or say that you would like to have done or said, or the things that you said that you wished you hadn't. The following morning, at the first opportunity, read the previous night's entry aloud to yourself in front of a full-length mirror to observe your body language. Do it regularly and you'll notice the confidence in your self-expression grow.

○ Two 1s

Blessed with the gift of balanced self-expression, people with two 1s are the most fortunate people. It is a valuable Birth Chart characteristic that should always be used wisely – never abuse it for manipulative purposes. (Always take care to avoid intolerance of people who are not so fortunate, especially if you are in love with someone without two 1s.)

The person with two 1s is often able to see both sides of a situation or argument, and it is not uncommon for them to take the other side midway through a discussion if it should suddenly appear more valid. This makes for an extremely broad understanding of situations and people.

Many successful politicians and other public figures are found to have two 1s. It tends to heighten humanitarian awareness and expression, and the ability to see both sides of any problem.

○ THEE 1s

There are two distinctly different types of expression here. The most frequently encountered is the talkative type, the chatterbox who is invariably bright and interesting and likes to be involved in many and varied activities. They generally find life enjoyable and seek to share that enjoyment with others.

The second group comprises a minority who also have no numbers on the Soul Plane. They are generally quiet, somewhat introspective and occasionally shy, especially with strangers. However, they do tend to become perky and talkative in friendly company when they feel at ease. These people find they can express themselves better through writing, where their thoughts flow more freely, uninhibited by their acute sensitivity.

○ FOUR 1s

People with four 1s experience difficulty with verbal expression and are therefore often misunderstood. But life soon teaches them to hide emotional turmoil with a smile, though they tend to suffer inwardly unless they learn to release such emotions and not strongly identify with them.

A strong egocentricity, these people identify with those for whom they share deep feelings. But they do not easily verbalise such feelings. For their personal happiness and that of the people who are close to them, it is important for people with four 1s to take command of their emotions. As they relax more and improve in self-confidence, they will feel less inhibited and become freer to express rather than suppress their inner feelings.

○ FIVE OR MORE 1s

With five, six or seven 1s on the Birth Chart, ego suppression is created to counteract the basic difficulty with verbal expression. Young can indeed be quite sad as they are often misunderstood. This creates aloofness, which leads in turn to increasing loneliness. They can become somewhat obsessive about their appearances and actions and often have lots of mirrors at home, which they tend to cover lest people should think them egocentric. Yet they secretly adore looking at themselves. Such egoism and deception can readily lead to mental imbalances.

You can help children with multiple 1s elevate their consciousness by getting them involved in an artform such as writing, painting, pottery or music, and so on. This applies to all children irrespective of age.

The occurrence of seven 1s in a birth date is extremely rare, fortunately appearing no more than once a century throught the 20th century

o NUMBER 2

Located at the gateway of the Soul Plane, 2 is the key to intuition, sensitivity and feeling. After the number 1 and 9, 2 is the most common found in birth dates of the 20th century, and will clearly be the most common number of the 21st century.

To possess a 2 on your Birth Chart is indeed a blessing for it provides you with a valuable guide to the degree of your sensitivity and intuition. As these faculties develop, you acquire an enhanced understanding of yourself, other people, life and all creation.

As those born in the 21st century grow to maturity and take increased responsibility in human affairs, the 20th century's headlong crusade into egocentricity and ambition will give way to intuitive sensitivity to world affairs. We'll also witness greater honour and fairness in business dealings, and increased concern in domestic affairs and friendships.

Meanwhile, do not assume that birth dates without a number 2 indicate a total absence of intuition and sensitivity. Rather it simply suggests that these traits need to be developed.

o ONE 2

Birth Charts with a single 2 indicate a sound, basic level of intuition – but not always enough in this highly competitive world, especially for men. With so much emphasis on artificial values in social, artistic and commercial expression today, individuals must be "tuned in" to successfully compete. And this cannot be properly achieved without a high degree of balanced sensitivity. Without the balance, sensitive natures can be easily hurt, often resulting in unwise reactions. This is more so with men than with women.

A single 2 provides a valuable foundation for developing balanced sensitivity, but the balanced double 2 offers the ideal qualities. Women possess a "de facto" 2 on their Birth Chart, for their very natures are more highly sensitive and intuitive than that of men. Thus, with a single 2 on their Birth Chart, women are blessed with the equivalent of the balanced double 2, whereas men have to diligently practise developing balanced sensitivity, their single 2 a great starting point.

In general, people with one 2 on their Birth Chart have found that they need ample time to relax and spend time in nature away from the intensity of competitive living. An individual's Ruling Number is the most reliable guide for how to do this (see Chapter 7).

○ Two 2s

As already explained, the balance of the second 2 on the Birth Chart is a great advantage, providing the ideal quality for the easy development of intuitive sensitivity. Even so, people with two 2s must use it appropriately and recognise that any virtue not used invariably deteriorates.

An innate perception endows these people with an intelligence that is above the average, based on an acute natural ability to understand people and circumstances. They possess an amazingly reliable guide when it comes to first impressions, almost instant and accurate opinions of people and concepts are often made. Sincerity or insincerity in others is thereby easily detected, so long as their ego and imagination do not interfere and colour their basic intuition.

The balanced intuitive sensitivity of these people (if positively expressed) tends to draw them to become involved in many aspects of human affairs. They generally do so with significant success, but need to guard against the tendency of becoming too available for too many worthy causes. This could be to the detriment of their personal happiness at home. As always, balance is the key to their success.

○ THREE 2s

Once we move beyond the "beam of the balance," as Pythagoras symbolically phrased it, we uncover excess. Three 2s on a Birth Chart indicates an unbalanced sensitivity, a hypersensitivity that can become quite an emotional load to carry for some people. It indicates that the person is highly attuned to the feelings of others, resulting in a ready inclination to become deeply involved in other people's problems.

As a form of sensitive self-protection, these people have the tendency to spend much of their time in a world of their own feelings, thereby exhibiting an aloofness that can lead to loneliness.

Many people with three 2s work in the entertainment field where they achieve remarkable success, sensitively portraying other characters. However, difficulty in expressing deep personal feelings also arises from such sensitivity, leading to hurts. They then tend to become defensive and impulsively say hurtful things.

Children with three 2s often become great imitators as it is so natural for them to share the sensitivities and feelings of others without realising it. However, success coping with life's emotional roller coaster will be largely under the charge of their parents, whose most constructive role is to assist their children to achieve a solid basis of self-confidence, in line with the path indicated by the child's Ruling Number (see Chapter 7).

○ FOUR 2s

Such a high level of impressionability has to be carefully and contin-
uously disciplined or it will easily erupt into severe misrepresenta-
tions, invariably accompanied by bad temper, sarcasm and spite.
These people are often extremely impatient. Their intuition becomes
unreliable as they misinterpret so much, and their confusion tends
to place their confidence in the wrong people. They invariably overreact and become quite volatile and emotionally unbalanced.

Extreme patience and understanding needs to be shown by family and friends (of which they rarely have too many). Though people
with four 2s comprise only a very small proportion of the population,
they feature highly in marital break-ups and bankruptcies, or homes
for handicapped people. They rarely make high public office, yet
when they do find it difficult to be considered credible, thus sinking
to the bottom quicker than they rose unless they have some highly
influential family strings to pull.

The lives of people with four 2s are often very lonely, and many
turn to drugs, alcohol and other substances or habits. They can
avoid such emotional isolation if they open themselves up to wise
and appropriate counselling. They need to learn to firmly apply
self-control when it comes to emotional expression, to relax and
meditate as needed and flow with the movement of life rather than
be at variance with it.

○ FIVE 2s

This is an extremely rare occurrence; it last occurred on 12/22/2002.
I've only met one person with such a birth date and, though it was
in a business environment, it was clear that the person was hiding a
deep heartache and was confused in his own personal life. This confusion carried over into his business decision making and resulted in
unnecessary bankruptcy not long after.

Individuals with five 2s are very likely to become totally reactive to their enormous sensitivity. They need extremely concentrated and devoted care and guidance, especially when very young, and they will try another's patience to the ultimate.

Not only will more birth dates occur with five 2s in this millennium, but we will also find the occasional six 2s, the first born on 2/22/2022, and the rare seven 2s – 2/22/2222 and 12/22/2222 (may this book be in print so long). In the last century, Birth Charts with five 2s also had at least a 1 and a 9, but in this millennium individuals with six or seven 2s will not have such a minor counterbalance, so will need extraordinarily special counselling and care (right from infancy if possible) when it comes to emotional expression.

○ NUMBER 3

Not only is this the gateway number to the Mind Plane, but it is also the most essential of the mind numbers for it governs memory. Whereas with 1s and 2s the most ideal balance and power were found when either was represented on the Birth Chart as a pair, with the 3 and higher numbers, right up to 9, the single number indicates the most desirable strength for itself and to assist balanced power elsewhere in the Birth Chart.

Absence of the number 3 on the Birth Chart does not imply mental weakness unless the person succumbs to laziness and or indifference. Generally, it indicates that the person needs to exert greater effort in the mental spheres, especially if their Ruling Number is not a mind number (see Chapter 7), or their sun sign is not a head sign (see Chapter 12). However, the tendency towards laziness when the 3 is absent must be recognised and corrected in the younger years, or else it will create great difficulties in later years.

○ ONE 3

As the anchor of memory, the single 3 on the Birth Chart provides a natural quality that will capably support people with it throughout life, so long as it is maintained (any faculty not used will atrophy). This 3 makes it easy for them to maintain alert mental activity.

The power of the 3 is a great natural aid to the young. It will assist them with their education, formally and informally. They will maintain an active interest in life and the environment.

As mental strength and agility are vital foundations for the cultivation of a balanced and optimistic understanding of life, these people generally have happy dispositions and can readily apply themselves successfully to most tasks. They usually possess an above average level of self-confidence, which also contributes to their success in life.

○ TWO 3s

With this increased mental alertness comes a pronounced accentuation of one's imagination and increased literary ability. Such power has to be carefully disciplined to facilitate its most useful and most balanced expression, and to avoid what might become antisocial behaviour if allowed to run riot.

To facilitate self-discipline, the practice of meditation is valuable, together with memory training and the development of intuition. This enables the development of more constructive thought processes. Otherwise, the highly active brain of the two 3s will place too much emphasis on imagination to the detriment of objective planning, investigation and positive comprehension. In so doing, they tend to lose tract of reality.

Most people with two or three 3s on their Birth Charts have significant writing ability, though they rarely realise this without outside help. They need to be encouraged to set their thoughts and imaginings on paper, for this will stimulate a free-flowing literary expression. In turn, such expression will help these people channel this potentially rampant quality, and perhaps readily turn it into a lucrative source of income.

○ THREE 3s

With even greater emphasis on mental activity and expression, these people often lose contact with reality, resulting in isolation that brings loneliness. They create their own "reality," but unfortunately no one else sees it that way, thereby contributing to their isolation. Their fertile imagination is so intent on thinking ahead and conceiving weird scenarios that they often find it difficult to focus on the present and relate to other people.

With such an overbalance, these people find trust difficult to accept, are rarely relaxed and may become addicted to stress-relieving drugs. Close friendships are rare for them and happiness is very much a stranger in their lives. They are sometimes so absorbed in their mental adventures that they become oblivious to everything around them, which can be quite disconcerting when people are talking to them. Such unbalanced concentration does not equip these people to see things in their true perspective. Their introversion exacerbates their distrust of other people, often leading to argumentativeness.

That these people need patient, understanding and caring assistance is patently obvious. The best way to provide this is to encourage them to focus on the present moment. They need to be taught practicality through the conscious application of their hands and hearts to manual activity of an artistic nature. Patience and understanding on the part of the helper must ultimately prevail.

○ Four 3s

This unusual amount of 3s can only occur during one month of any century – it last transpired on 3/31/1933 and will not occur again until 3/3/2033.

The excessive imagination and mental hyperactivity of these people can bring them to the point of intense fear, worry and confusion. They have little or no regard for physical concerns, with a terribly impractical outlook on life in general.

As understanding them demands so much of others, they rarely have close friends. Yet that is exactly what they need, most especially someone who will help withdraw their attention from the intensely mental toward more practical concerns. There is no other way by which they will become balanced or happy individuals. The phobias and obsessions plaguing the person with four 3s will only intensify if they are acknowledged as real. Such attitudes must be shown for what they are – figments of the imagination that clearly indicate sever deficiencies in these people's means of expression. They need to be encouraged and taught practical activities, such as dressmaking, hairdressing, landscaping, interior decorating and writing. They must become involved in the "doing" side of life.

○ Number 4

Symbolically, the 4 represents containment and regularity as depicted by the square. It is a practical and material number, located squarely in the centre of the Physical Plane of the Birth Chart. People with this number are generally tidy and meticulous, practical and organised.

Birth Charts without a 4 indicate a degree of impatience in the person, but the degree to which this prevails depends significantly upon other numerological factors, such as Ruling Number, Day Number and Arrows. For example, if they also possess the Arrow of the Intellect, they will be impatient with people who do not speedily grasp explanations or concepts. If they have the Arrow of Emotional Balance they will be impatient with people who do not keep their emotions under control. Such an impatient disposition can be largely overcome by conscious attention to detail and by care and concern for other people's needs.

○ ONE 4

These are active people who express a natural identity with the practical, including organisational, technical, financial and or physical involvements (gardening, manual arts, building, and so on). Their most fluent avenue of expression will be generally indicated by their Ruling Number (see Chapter 7).

Preferring to work with concrete rather than theoretical concepts, these people are often sceptical when it comes to obscure theories. They prefer practice to principles and become impatient with unwarranted delays and procrastination. They want to get on with the task at hand, and will become especially dogmatic about this is they also possess a number 7 on the Birth Chart.

Too much emphasis on the physical can make them somewhat materialistic. This is a negative aspect of the 4, and its intention if to teach them to use their natural patience to avoid extreme materialism, best achieved through the development of care and compassion for others. Only in this way will they attain lasting friendship and happiness.

○ TWO 4s

The double 4 can lead to an unbalanced outlook that relates everything to the physical and material. The powerful utilitarian aspect of these people must seek balanced expression between the physical, mental and spiritual. This allows them to learn to identify and be in harmony with their thoughts and feelings.

If their Ruling Number is spiritual or mental (see Chapter 7), these people will have a greater natural ability to rise above the physical than if their Ruling Number were also physical. A well-chosen name will also be of considerable help to achieve balance (see Chapter 13).

The more 4s on the Birth Chart, the greater the need for balance to be developed, and greater care must be exercised in choosing friends. They should especially endeavour to steer clear of the hard-drinking, heavy-smoking type of person, for they require far more sensitivity from friends and colleagues if they are to be successful in developing balance in their lives. These people will benefit from the company of others who enjoy the aesthetic and cultural qualities of life.

○ THREE 4s

All the aspects of the double 4 prevail here, only with greater intensity, for these people experience even greater difficulty rising above the physical, and even when they do, they are so often drawn back by materialism. Those who recognise this pull to materialism must employ great effort of will and be receptive to dedicated, caring guidance.

Many people with this aspect feel the constant pull toward hard, manual work and persist with it to the point of exhaustion, not realising that their lesson is the mastery of it, rather than enslavement to it. Only such mastery do they acquire the desirable balance between the physical and mental and spiritual expression. They must guard against relating everything to the physical and going overboard about such concerns as neatness.

People with three or four 4s have a tendency toward weak lower limbs, for they place a lot of emphasis on the legs. They should take exceptional care of their knees, ankles and feet.

○ FOUR 4s

This is another extremely rare occurrence; it last happened on 4/24/1944 and will next occur on 4/4/2044.

Due to the extreme pull of the physical, extreme care in all activities must be taken. There exists a critical weakness in their lower limbs, which for many will result in temporary or permanent crippling.

All the advice and help suggested for those with three 4s applies even more so when four 4s appear on the Birth Chart. Extreme patience is demanded with these people; as they are so highly sceptical of non-physical (metaphysical) concepts you can easily become bored with their one-eyed pragmatism.

○ NUMBER 5

The unique position of this number in the centre of the Birth Chart demands special attention for it governs the intensity of human feelings like no other influence on the Birth Chart. As the second number on the Soul (Feeling) Plane, 5 is the numerological equivalent of the heart chakra for it symbolises love and freedom of expression, emotionally and artistically.

It is the only number on the Birth Chart to have direct contact with every other number. Its "symbolic love" influence enhances the expression of every quality in life as expressed by the other numbers. Its other unique factor is its containment, being completely "boxed in" and surrounded, whereas each of the other eight numbers is open to the universe. At first glance, this might appear a paradox for the number that represents freedom, but it actually indicates how freedom must be attained – by dismantling rigid barriers that seek to entrap humans.

○ ONE 5

With the single 5 in the centre of the Birth Chart, the best chance of achieving a balanced personality becomes available. It is also the only number that ensures none of the corner numbers take on their isolated qualities (as explained at the end of this chapter). In particular, the single 5 greatly assists the individual to achieve emotional control, for it ensures that their sensitivity to life develops as a reliable intuitive guide. This allows them to become more adept at choosing suitable courses of action, rather than responding to situations through thoughtless reaction.

As a valuable protection to sensitivity, the single 5 strengthens fortitude and compassion, thereby creating what we have come to regard as strength of character. It also provides the power of love and freedom that enhances all other forms of expression. The single 5 assists the individual to understand their own feelings and so enhances a deep appreciation for the feelings of others.

○ TWO 5s

People with this concentration of 5s are frequently recognised for their driving intensity. The outward reflection of this vigour is invariably expressed in their powerful, staring eyes and furrowed brows. Intensified determination gives them an air of great confidence and self-assurance, which can often be more wishful than factual. As they mature, this self-assurance tends to diminish to mere bravado and they find it difficult to cope with the intense emotional, domestic and vocational troubles that emerge in their lives from time to time. They must watch the tendency to over-intensify these troubles and magnify them out of all proportion.

The drive and enthusiasm of these people can at times become overbearing and the cause of misunderstandings – to the annoyance and exasperation of the people close to them. So intense are they in the expression of their attitudes that they often create emotional turmoil in their environment and, develop digestive ulcers and associated health problems in the region of the solar plexus. They regularly suffer from indigestion; for many it has prevailed for so long and become so chronic that they hardly seem to realise they have it, except for the intestinal gas, constipation and stomach distension.

Special care should be taken by these people to exercise emotional control, or they could easily become dependent on drugs or sex for the relief and or release of their pent-up emotional energy. Preceding meal times, they must make certain that their emotions do not take charge, or they will suffer from acute digestion soon after the meal. A hot cup of naturally-soothing herb tea, such as chamomile, sipped about half an hour before the meal, plus some soft relaxing music during the meal, will be greatly beneficial to them (and, for that matter, to everyone).

○ THREE 5s

Points made for the double 5 are even more intensified when a person has three 5s on their Birth Chart. Such emotional intensity as this can be very difficult for many people to handle. Fortunately, few are born with this extreme intensity of drive and feeling.

Very special and careful training in self-discipline has to be a vital part of the early lives of these people. This places unique responsibility on the parents who, rarely equipped for such a task, often feel lost in failing to understand their complex child. Parents should not despair; as their love and understanding wins through, they will realise how much they have learned from the experience.

For both parents and child, thinking before speaking or acting will enable the influence of wisdom to prevail and will avoid offending the sensitivity of such intense people. As a consequence, they will not then need to erect a barrier to protect their sensitivity, which more effectively ruins their social life and happiness.

○ Four 5s

This occurs as rarely as the four 3s and 4s, fortunately. The last person to be born with four 5s was on 25/5/1955, and the next birth will not occur until 5/5/2055.

The overwhelming intensity of feeling and sensitivity within the solar plexus of these people can be almost life-threatening. They are highly accident prone and generally in a state of advanced stress. Life has the habit of inflicting upon us "accidents" to either slow us down or to turn us around if we have digressed from the Path. But if we do not re-assess our situation, we may find more intense "accidents" strewn along our path. This is typical of person with four 5s.

Life for these people can be very difficult to understand if they do not permit wise guidance to direct them.

○ Number 6

Located in the centre of the Mind Plane, the number 6 represents human creativity as well as its opposite, destruction. The choice is always ours as to whether we embrace the positive or negative aspects of a number, but from 6 through to 9, the divergence between the two aspects becomes more pronounced.

Creativity is probably best understood as "the activity of the Creator." And because we are microscopic (minute) aspects of the macrocosmic (gigantic) power, the faculty of that same creativity (albeit in a much attenuated form) is inherent within us all. The 6 provides the creative link between the 3 of memory and analysis (left brain) and the 9 of responsible idealism (right brain); it facilitates the smooth and constructive working of the Mind Plane.

The number 6 is also located at the head of the Arrow of the Will (see Chapter 6), and as such brings the will into harmony with the mind. This is achieved with the support of the practical love of the 4 and the love of the 5 underpinning it.

Birth Charts with no number 6 indicate the need for the person to consciously develop their creative faculties through the powers of their existing numbers. If they possess a 3, the task is made easier. Without the aid of the 3, they must employ more diligent mental effort to produce the creativity necessary for the development of their individuality.

○ ONE 6

The number of creativity, it finds its most common expression in the deep love of the home. However, its more personal expression can be found in the artistic fields, such as pottery, painting, composing, acting, and similar disciplines.

People with one 6 have a strong focus on domestic responsibility, which tends to mask the true role of the 6, creative expression. However, as these people become more aware and mature, they will find that domestic satisfaction alone leaves much to be desired. It is then that they will exert their strength of will to bring more expressive personal creativity into their lives – or they will continue to wonder why they are not receiving sufficient fulfilment from their life's endeavours. As they "discover" the arts and especially the creative power of music, their lives will blossom amazingly.

○ TWO 6s

The double 6 can be either a mighty challenge or a heavy handi-cap. How the individual handles it depends on many factors, such as their Ruling Number and environmental factors, particularly the early influence of their parents.

With less aware people, the negative aspects will be initially inclined to prevail. These produce worry, anxiety, stress and irritability, particularly around the home and place of work. Loved ones feel this negativity most and for all involved it can produce nervous upsets and illness. This is best counteracted by directing interests beyond the limitations of the home into areas of creative expression. This is not to say that they should neglect their homes, or that their homes are not already a place of creative expression (they are vital expressions of their loving care), they simply need to expand their focus to include more personally creative pursuits. Their vocation must be a creative one, inspired by confident and understanding direction. They must be guided, never pushed or threatened. Love and appreciation are vital to them, acting as balm to their alert nervous systems.

These people require much more rest than most, for they use so much nervous energy in their creative or everyday pursuits. They must learn to meditate before going to bed to ensure that their sleep is deeply restful. When possible, and if desired, they should take the time for an afternoon siesta.

○ THREE 6S

With the extra 6 on the Birth Chart comes greater worry concerning the home, worry that is of the individual's own making, a consequence of domestic confusion. Women suffer more, for they usually do not seek to be involved in anything outside the home. As such, they become fanatically protective and possessively loving.

The problem with so many people with this power is that they rarely realise its positive potential for brilliant creativity. Instead, they turn it inward upon themselves and it becomes a tornado of disturbed emotions. Their acute over-protectiveness of their children is indicative of this. They secretly fear their children growing up and eventually leaving home, creating an unhealthy possessiveness that ultimately drives the children away from the home earlier than might have otherwise occurred.

Special care must be taken to achieve balance in their lives. Adequate rest, creative expression and care with diet will provide the appropriate corrective measures.

○ FOUR 6S

Four 6s on a Birth Chart only occurs thrice a century, the last being 6/26/1966, which at least had the additional numbers 1, 2 and 9 on the Birth Chart to provide some relief. But the next birth date with four 6s occurs on 6/26/2066, and only provides two 2s as additional help, thereby focusing even more strongly on the enormously heavy burden of the four 6s.

While four 6s indicates exceptional creative potential, the negative aspect, as stimulated by the emotions, is ever-ready to dominate. As such, these people are likely to become pathetic worriers, virtually sabotaging their health and their friendships because of endless complaining. This is, of course, unless their parents have recognised this tendency in the child's early years and have lovingly and patiently guided their child's creative potential. The positive expression of the four 6s can be easily achieved with unconditional love.

○ NUMBER 7

As the highest number of the Physical Plane, 7 represents a special function of human life. It indicates the amount of learning one must amass, generally through that unforgettable form of personal experience called sacrifice. Its deeper, philosophical significance lies in two domains, physically, 7 represents practical activity as the means for consummate learning and teaching; spiritually, 7 is the "temple" number, the repository of philosophy, truth and wisdom. This further indicates the need to detach from worldly possessions in order to integrate body and soul.

Sacrifice is not to be avoided; it's a wonderful opportunity for cleansing and refining. It is when we fail to practise sacrifice voluntarily that the universe sees to it that such "purification" takes place. It's best to take control of what we sacrifice in our lives, that way we are more aware of the ultimate purpose of the experience, rather than lamenting it as an undesirable lesson.

Lack of 7 on the Birth Chart reveals that either the person has evolved through that form of sacrifice in recent past lives and is no longer in need of that type of learning (except during the Personal Year of 7, which we all experience, or the Pyramid Peak of 7). Alternatively and more commonly, it implies that the person does not have the necessary philosophical understanding of sacrifice and has to put practical effort into achieving it.

○ ONE 7

As part of the vital learning process of life, sacrifices in matters of health, love, money or possessions will be encountered when this number appears on the Birth Chart. This is only intended as part of the soul's unfolding. The resultant sacrifices are often bemoaned by the sufferers without realising the vital role of "giving up to acquire." As we release our identity with physical possessions, we learn the difference between "preference" and "obsession." So far as health and love are concerned, any loss in these areas is intended to strengthen and purify our habits and attitudes. If we are to fulfil our purpose here on Earth, we must ensure our health is properly nourished. In love, all too often we confuse desire with unconditional love. Remember, we can never lose if we practise unconditional love, but we rarely retain love when we associate it with emotional demands and expectations.

○ Two 7s

Two 7s clearly implies the intensity of the lessons to be undertaken. We invariably find that the lessons occur through loss in two of the three basic areas of life: health, love or money possessions. The intensity of the experience involving sacrifice is intended to focus the individual upon the deeper philosophical understanding of life. This stimulates our interest in the metaphysical, with which comes enlightened powers for healing, guidance and compassion.

When not living positively, these people fail to develop that indispensable philosophical understanding of life, which they are so capable. Instead, they constantly complain about loss, blame others for their problems, and accuse life of being grossly unfair and handing them a dirty deal. They become grumpy, pitiful individuals that most people prefer to avoid.

○ THREE 7s

Superficially, three 7s in a Birth Chart appears to result in particularly sad lives brought about by heavy loss in all three areas of life: health, love and money possessions. But the sadness is often more unsettling to the close associate than it is to the sufferer who, with such a depth of philosophical understanding, recognises the purpose behind the events.

Such loss tests these people's powers of fortitude and compassion, endowing them with enormous strength of character. This can make for a truly remarkable person, a valuable friend whose outlook on life grows with maturity, displaying almost infinite depths of wisdom. Such is only the case with those people with three 7s who recognise opportunity in every challenge.

For those negative souls who prefer to languish in the mud-holes of life and rely on sympathy to justify their existence, the tendency toward depression and anti-social behaviour loses them many friends and further exacerbates their problems.

○ Four 7s

Lecturing in Toronto, Canada, during the month of July 1977, I felt deep compassion for the infants born on 7, 17 and 27 July, as well as for the parents who had no idea of the problems they would need to face with such children. Unexpectedly, I received word from a dear friend of mine back home in Sydney that he had become the proud father of a first born on 7/27/1977, and what problems they have all experienced since. Fortunately, no more souls will incarnate with four 7s until 7/7/2077.

To both the children and the parents of the children with four 7s, exceedingly careful help is necessary, else all will feel the burden of such compounded sacrifice. Yet, once understood, as I have endeavoured to explain here, it can be an exciting learning experience. A change in attitude is necessary to see the half-full rather than the half-empty glass.

The heightened philosophical understanding that attends such a life provides wonderful potential for rapid growth in spiritual consciousness. But certain basic training is necessary for this to occur, the training being in the form of essential personal disciplines by which the person learns to gain "empire over the self," as Pythagoras so eloquently phrased it.

○ Number 8

As the most active number of the Soul Plane, 8 exerts a dual influence. Spiritually, it is the number of wisdom; physically, it is the number of active independence.

Symbolically, 8 appears as the double 4, the double square, one atop the other. This elevates some of the organisational and practical aspects of the 4 onto the higher plane of expression, revealing the close affinity between the 4 and 8, though they are on totally different planes.

Birth Charts without an 8 indicate that those people have to deliberately apply themselves to achieve that desirable level of wisdom and independence that makes life more fulfilling and rewarding.

○ ONE 8

These people are most methodical and meticulous when living positively. On the other hand, apathy and instability prevail when they exist negatively.

Tidiness, with considerable attention to detail and a feel for efficiency, is natural to these people. These are the aspects of practical wisdom that underlie their development in independence. However, if these people choose the negative path, they become emotionally unstable, reactive and restless, resulting in frequent changes in home, career or relationships.

○ TWO 8s

The sharpened power of assessment of the two 8s on the Birth Chart can be either extremely beneficial or highly unsettling, depending on how positive the individual is. In matters demanding special care to detail, these people can excel like few others. But they must beware that their perceptiveness does not allow them to become dictatorial from overconfidence. This would give rise to inward emotional conflict, resulting in instability and extreme restlessness.

Their search for truth and wisdom can stimulate such restlessness, but in a positive manner. It inspires them to travel which, we must realise, is a wonderful source of knowledge and wisdom. If they do not travel when they are young, deep frustration can develop that exacerbates their irritability. This can lead to a feeling of confinement, and only when travel opportunities are fulfilled do they eventually find some semblance of peace of mind.

○ THREE 8s

The acute restlessness induced by the negative aspect of three 8s is more frequently met than its opposite. To feel that life is pointless and frustrating is to be a victim of the most extreme pessimism. So these people need considerable love and guidance to encourage them to adopt a largely positive outlook on life. After all, they must realise that life goes on whether or not they are positive and enjoying it. All they have to do is change their attitude and join the swim, rather than bemoan the temperature of the water they haven't even tried.

For the positive person with three 8s, great wisdom and that glorious feeling of independence underpins their daily living. Even though they prefer to be on the go, they have an inner stability and a joyousness that wins them many friends. Unfortunately, only a minority live this way, though it is to be hoped that this advice will win more converts.

○ FOUR 8s

The last person to be born with four 8s was on 8/28/1988, and the next such birth will not occur until 8/8/2088.

They will be extremely hyperactive, restless people. As infants and children, they should never be forced to sit and watch television or told to "sit still," for this unnaturalness (for them) will only lead to excessive frustration and, ultimately, quite irrational behaviour from pent-up emotions. They should be taught to develop a sound sense of direction and be taken places as often as possible until they are old enough to travel on their own.

○ NUMBER 9

A most powerful number, the Romans regarded it as the war number, symbolising the planet Mars. We know it to be a number of war *and* prosperity, but so much depends on how it is used. As the number symbolising mental activity, 9 is also representative of the right lobe of our brain and its power of idealism, its spiritual component.

Its physical counterpart manifests as ambition and it is just that power that caused so much international strife and confusion in the world in the 20th century.

From the beginning of this century, more people have been born without a 9 on their Birth Chart At the same time, everyone will have at least one 2 on their Birth Chart, thereby greatly transfer-ring the emphasis from the Mind to the Soul Plane. In summary, more people will have deep feelings and there will be less egocen-tric ambitiousness. However, this will not become significantly apparent until closer to the middle of this century, when those born at its beginning will be mature and responsible enough to take the reigns of decision making.

○ ONE 9

Ambition, responsibility and idealism – these are the three major qualities of the 9. This power has been at the foundation of humanity's driving force for the past century, responsible for our drive to find out more about life and to control it more. Not that it appears to have succeeded very well Though we know infinitely more about our environment and what it is to be human than we did at the beginning of the 20th century, we also have more envi-ronmental degradation, human sickness and suffering and exten-sive famine and poverty than at any time in the past two centuries. What went wrong? Could it be that too much focus was put on ambition and not enough on responsibility and idealism?

The most beneficial application of one 9 on the Birth Chart is to express it through balance of the three aspects. Any fanaticism to overcompensate for past errors or omissions can only lead to further reactions. The practice of temperance is vital here: "moderation in all things suitable, abstention from those unsuitable," as Pythagoras taught.

○ Two 9s

An intensity of idealism and zeal, coupled with serious thought, characterises these people. They often express such an overzealous idealism that it becomes quite impractical to implement. They must be careful to maintain a sound level of practicality to balance the idealism.

The inclination to become critical of others with a lower level of idealistic intensity must be guarded against and overcome if they are to find happiness in life. Yet these people are deep thinkers, and at the heart of all they do they wish to be helpful. It just needs to be clearly expressed and not expected to be taken for granted.

○ Three 9s

The exceptional power of idealism and ambition of the three 9s is extremely difficult to handle and can at times produce mental imbalance with those who do not realise their power. This problem can be avoided by recognising the three 9s in the Birth Charts of children and training them to balance their expression more evenly over the three Planes than so powerfully through the Mind Plane.

It is not uncommon for these people, when acting negatively, to allow small things to become exaggerated out of all proportion. This often results in outbursts of temper, leading to loss of emotional control, even to the extent of threatening mental balance.

The vital lesson here is to look at all things objectively and in proportion to their real value. This will help dissolve their judgement and permit the acceptance of small deviations from their rigid idealism.

○ Four 9s

From time to time we come across people born with four 9s on their Birth Chart. Though they comprise only a small fraction of the population, they invariably need help. Among them we generally find two distinct types.

The most common, especially with the advent of modern "hippy-ism" are those who live in a dream world of vague unreality. They have often dropped out of society because they could not come to grips with what didn't confer with their fanatical idealism. Some are not like this consistently. They appear to be "normal" and conforming until, from time to time, they can take it no more and either take themselves far away or lock themselves in their homes for days or months on end. But these are quite harmless people who deny that anything is wrong with them and do not respond well to guidance.

The other type are those who adopt an aggressive, somewhat belligerent attitude and appear to take pleasure in belittling others, who, in their opinion, fall so far short of their ideals. These can be the dangerous ones and should receive wise counselling before they become irreversibly lonely or do harm to themselves or someone else in a fit of rage.

○ Five 9s

A few infants with five 9s came into this world during September of the last year of the 20th century. Understanding them will be almost an impossibility without the aid of numerology, and even then, helping them will be another even greater challenge.

Everything written about those with four 9s applies to the five 9s, only with compounded significance. It is to be hoped that their parents are highly trained numerologists, for teaching them to be practical and compassionate will be the greatest challenge.

○ *The isolated numbers*

Many Birth Charts of the 20th century will have more empty spaces than full, a situation that becomes even more pronounced in the 21st century. This will often lead to the isolation of one or more of the corner numbers of the Birth Chart (1, 3, 7 and 9). These isolated numbers have special significance for people with who have them on their Birth Charts.

○ ISOLATED 1s

When the numbers 2, 5 and 4 are missing from a Birth Chart, the number 1 will be isolated from all other numbers. As "1" is the number symbolising the expression of the human ego, its isolation on the Birth Chart reveals why these people so often feel isolated and misunderstood when they try to explain their feelings to others, especially if they have a single 1. Such Birth Charts will have a heavy concentration of numbers either on the Mind Plane and/or on the Arrow of Activity . A heavy concentration of numbers on the Arrow of Activity indicates that the person has trouble clearly explaining to others the concepts and or actions they choose to undertake.

If their numbers are more heavily concentrated on the Mind Plane, the person might be perceived as lazy or unreliable because so much going on in their head won't get translated into practical expression, or because they make commitments to do things that rarely get done. This can lead others to think that people with isolated 1s are unreliable when, if effect, they are mostly unaware of this aspect of their nature. Unless it is corrected, it can lead to loneliness so that the isolated ego magnifies into an isolated person.

Correction is easy. For every isolated number, the one quality missing that will integrate the Birth Chart and "de-isolate" each number is that represented by the number 5 in the centre of the Birth Chart. Generally, this implies the need for any person who has one or more isolated numbers to develop more love and compassion in their expression, and to learn to more freely express their positive emotions rather than bottle them up. When only the 1 is isolated, developing the qualities indicated by the 2 or the 4 can also help. For example developing the intuition of the 2 so that the expression of the ego can be connected with the power of analysis (the 3), and practised with the improved logic, patience and practicality of the 4.

○ ISOLATED 3s

When a single 3 or compounded 3s are alone in the upper left of the Birth Chart, with the numbers 2, 5 and 6 missing, the person is recognised as having the "isolated-3" problem. This means that their strong mind potential can be easily diffused for it is unconnected with the Physical Plane and its powers are not readily carried through into practise. This problem can be severely compounded when more than one 3 is isolated, for then the imagination can run riot and these people can become either paranoid or "legends in their own minds."

Correction is similar to that employed for the isolated 1. The person needs to initially develop the power of the number 5 on their Birth Chart, as described above, followed by the development of their intuition through the power of the 2. This is similar to before, except that for the isolated 1 person logic had to be brought to the ego, now verbal expression has to be linked to the mind's power so that it can be given vent.

The third force desirous of development is that of the creative 6. This will link the 3 with the 9 (inherent in every birth date of the 20th century). Is so doing, the Arrow of Intellect (**see page ??**) is developed to give balance to the Mind Plane and the person's thinking abilities. Learning to embrace creative outlets is the best way to develop the 6 on the Birth Chart.

○ ISOLATED 7s

When one or more 7s occupy the lower right corner of the Birth Chart without a 4, 5 or 8 in contact with it them, the sacrifices and lessons to be learned by the person are generally necessarily repeated. The experience of learning has to be translated to the mind for its lesson to be recognised and understood. But when this learning area is isolated from the Mind Plane, the same or similar lessons have to be repeated until, by force of frequency, they become recognised. This implies that these people can lose in health, love or money possessions on repeated occasions until the appropriate lesson is brought home to them.

Though this is often hurtful to the sacrificing person, they tend to accept it as "fate" or inevitability. The hurt often seems worse to the friends and loved ones of the person who has to sacrificed. Remember, 7 is the number of philosophic understanding, so the person with the isolated 7 or 7s probably has more understanding of what has happened to them then those around them.

To minimise the hurt or sacrifice, the person needs to develop the powers inherent in the numbers 4, 5 and 8. We have already covered the qualities of the 4 and 5 with the forementioned isolated numbers, but now we see the development of the 4 helps the isolated 7 to unify with the ego expression of the 1 to feel okay about asking for help or guidance. At the same time, this develops the Arrow of Practicality so that the person develops a realistic approach to their life's experiences.

To develop the power of the 8 on the Birth Chart, the isolated 7 must become wiser when it comes applying practical intuition through loving action. This also helps to develop their sense of independence, and ultimately builds the Arrow of Activity. Here, the 5 and 8 work in total harmony, providing an excellent opportunity for the development of the person's Soul Plane.

○ ISOLATED 9s

When the numbers 5, 6 and 8 are missing from the Birth Chart, and the person has one or more 9s (as do all in the 20th century), the individual either exhibits impractical idealism, unrequited ambition, or both. This generally depends on the number of 9s on the Birth Chart. If a single 9, it is usually the sign of unfulfilled ambition; if a double 9, impractical idealism; if three or four 9s, both may prevail.

From the corrective measures recommended for the other isolated numbers, the technique is clearly easy to follow. In this case, the qualities of the 5, then the 6 and the 8 need to be inculcated into the person's expression. Of these, perhaps the 5 is the most important if the person does not have a 7 on their Birth Chart, for the five will link the 9/s with expression through the ego of the number 1. If they have a 7 as well, then the powers of both numbers (5 and 8) should be developed for optimum connection between the ambition idealism of the 9 and Physical Practical Plane.

○ *Summary*

Remember, the power of your original Birth Chart is not as important as what you do to fill its empty spaces. Some of the most successful people in history have had some of the weakest and emptiest Birth Charts. Their success has only come about by developing the qualities they lacked initially, and to evolve toward perfection, that is the purpose of life – Nothing can direct us better than numerology.

CHAPTER .06

The arrows of idividuality

*T*he more a numerologist practises the science, the more accurate their readings will become. With this accuracy comes a sharpening of intuition and greater speed at honing the most outstanding features of a person's individuality.

Experience teaches us that the first aspect of the Birth Chart we look for is the compounding of any numbers. This reveals particular strengths that the person is almost certain to have been drawing upon in the development of their personality. Then we look for missing numbers to ascertain the person's weaknesses The individual will either be seeking to overcome them or be using their strengths in an effort to hide them. After this comes our assessment of any Arrows present.

My teacher, Hettie Templeton, called them Arrows. It is uncertain whether Pythagoras ever used this pertinent aspect of numerology, though it would be surprising if he didn't. In the fragments of the original Science of Numbers that were faithfully reproduced by Philolaus, no reference to the Arrows, even by a different name, was found. Mrs T. learned of them during her teaching in the early part of the 20th century. She experimented with them – modified, expanded and developed them where she found the need – all in accordance with her decades of extensive experience.

My discovery of the Arrows during my time with Mrs T. opened up a whole new vista on the subject, for they so pertinently revealed deeper insights into the special aspects of human individuality. They brought a new depth of clarity and understanding.

The essence of the teachings of the Arrows follows. They are in accordance with the essential aspects of numerology; ie. each number has its unique roots in its Plane of expression. (Each number and its Plane are the first principles that provide the very foundation of the numerology to which we constantly refer whenever verification is required.)

Found in a few modern books on numerology are different interpretations of the Arrows, the consequence of the writers' wish to create variations, thereby avoiding copyright infringement. But in creating the differences, they have diffused and clouded the meanings of the Arrows. In some instances they have given "characteristics" that are totally misleading.

In calling them "Arrows," modern Pythagoreans want to create the impression that they highlight unique characteristics that make powerful observations regarding the individual.

Arrows are found on the Birth Chart where any three numbers exist in a straight line or where any three empty spaces exist in a straight line. Arrows of numbers are those of strength. Arrows of empty spaces are those of weakness, which can be overcome by using the strengths provided by the numbers on the Birth Chart.

ARROW OF DETERMINATION   *Birth date: 3.31.1950*

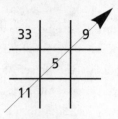

Everyone born during the month of May in the 20th century and everyone born on every day of the 1950s will have this Arrow on their Birth Chart so too will everyone born with a 5 anywhere else in their birth date. This is because the number 1 and 9 are standard to every birth date in the 20th century. Thus, only the 5 is needed to create the Arrow of Determination. Clearly, this has become the most prolific Arrow of the 20th century, so little wonder it has been such a century of achievement.

Determination underlies almost everything these people undertake. This is coupled with persistence, which is often used to overcome objections to their plans, sometimes to the point of dogged stubbornness. Some will want to enact their plans with all haste, others will go to the extreme of waiting until obstacles disperse. The middle path, employing their intuition, compassion and wisdom, will generally be the most suitable avenue.

One of the most difficult lessons for these people is to accept that not everything they determine is intended for them to do. So often they will regard obstacles as inconvenient stumbling blocks that must be overcome whatever the costs. Whereas, were they to use their intuition and wisdom, they would recognise if that were so or whether the obstacles were intended to divert them to another, more suitable course of action. This could avoid later disappointment or frustration.

DISCOVERING THE INNER SELF

The decisiveness of people with this Arrow can be a fine quality, it certainly is a powerful one. But they must learn to use it wisely rather than be motivated by stubbornness. This is particularly so if the Arrow is a compounded 1. It is not uncommon to find Birth Charts with two 1s, two 5s and two 9s, doubling the power of determination of this Arrow. This will demand even greater intuitive guidance for wise decision making before they leap headlong into a course of action they might later regret.

The direction of motivation indicated by this Arrow is generally toward the idealism or ambition of the 9 at its head when the Arrow comprises only single numbers. When any number is compounded, the focus of the Arrow is them directed toward that area of greatest strength. If there is a double 1 only, the focus is directed toward the ego's expression of determination; if a double 5 only, the focus is centred, with compassion or emotional freedom the prime motivators. If a double 9 heads the Arrow, the focus is directed toward the person's ambition or idealism, depending on their Ruling Number or other compounded numbers on the Birth Chart, if physical numbers dominate, the focus will be ambition; if spiritual or mental numbers dominate, the focus will be idealism.

Children with this Arrow express very decided tastes from infancy. They will need the space to freely express their strong determination, albeit with appropriate training in both understanding and moderation. They should never be driven against their wishes; they need to be led with loving kindness, and a firmness tempered by flexibility. They are generally quite intelligent children who will listen to reason but will question that reasoning if they perceive flaws in it. It is up to their parents and teachers to allow them ample opportunity to assert themselves, otherwise they could become very stubborn, which is reactive determination and not

54

conducive to a happy life. Their determination strengthens them for adult life so it should be nurtured whenever possible.

ARROW OF PROCRASTINATION   *Birth date: 4/3/2002*

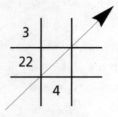

The presence of the Arrow of Procrastination effectively divides the Birth Chart in two, separating the intuitive analytical components from the practical. And so we experience procrastination, where things are delayed or not executed at all. This can be corrected in a young child, but if it is allowed to perpetuate, it will be extremely counter-productive to the person, inhibiting their progress in life and giving rise to constant frustration, both for the person and the people around them.

Caring parents should recognise this trait very early in their infant's life and teach them to develop the necessary patience and persistence to complete every little task the infant starts. Persistence and decisiveness need to be developed here and no opportunity should be overlooked to teach the child such lessons.

ARROW OF SPIRITUALITY   *Birth date: 7/6/1953*

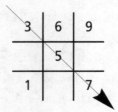

The Arrow formed by the second diagonal of numbers on the Birth Chart links the three most symbolically powerful numbers on each of the three Planes – the Mind 3, the Soul 5 and the Practical 7. These numbers are traditionally symbolic in many of the ancient mystery schools: 3 being the number of understanding of the Creative Principle; 5 the number of compassion in creative expression of the Principle; and 7 the sabbatical or rest day when the perfection of the Creator integrates with the philosophic and practical qualities of human creativity. It is interesting to note that most religions focus primarily on the number 3 alone (for example, Hinduism and Christianity), revealing their pre-occupation with the mental aspect of their teachings and the fear they often seek to cultivate in order to maintain the following of the faithful.

In its true essence, the linking of these three numbers creates the potential for a deep spiritual awareness that is the vital basis for a balanced practical philosophy on life. Such awareness encourages growth through personal experience because people with this Arrow of Spirituality generally prefer not to take advice from others. Where life's lessons are concerned, they much prefer practice to theory. This inclination will often bring sadness to their earlier lives, inspiring them to develop fortitude and further unfold their philosophic understanding of life.

With their profound experiences comes an inner power, a calmness and serenity that radiates from them, revealing their beautiful spirituality. It will often be said of them, "Their presence brings peace." And is that not exactly what is so often said of the Dalai Lama who has this Arrow? He was accorded a Nobel Peace Prize for having achieved that serenity and sharing it with so many others, even though his heart was breaking for his lost beloved homeland.

It is important to note that in the 20th century every Birth Chart with this Arrow of Spirituality also has the Arrow of Determination.

Thus, the two should be read together for the most thorough understanding of these powerful traits. During this millennium the conjoint occurrence of these two Arrows will be somewhat a rarity.

○ *Children* with the Arrow of Spirituality show an almost naive trust in people as well as a deep sense of natural justice. For this reason, they should never be wilfully deceived, but should be given a very special depth of love and care. If these children suspect their parents of deception, their trust will be shattered, their respect undermined and their own excuses for deceptive behaviour seemingly justified. They will become reactive, their comparatively peaceful disposition shaken.

It is important to carefully guide these children in spiritual matters, and to encourage them to learn about all religions and philosophies and to understand the ethical principles that ennoble human life. They have strong powers of perception, but often their immaturity inhibits their ability to evaluate and express what they feel and think. This can lead to frustration.

Encouragement to read well-chosen books, instead of watching violence on television is especially helpful when it comes to developing the spiritual awareness of these children. It is never too early to commence the awareness of their latent psychic faculties, such as intuition and extra-sensory perception (ESP), though it will often be found that these children are more psychically aware than their parents, lacking only the understanding and expression of their profound psychic powers.

ARROW OF THE ENQUIRER   *Birth date: 2/20/1981*

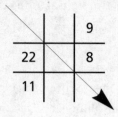

This arrow is ostensibly one of weakness, formed by the missing numbers 3, 5 and 7. It was originally taught to me as the Arrow of Scepticism, but my extensive observations over the past fifteen years have revealed that it is something even more than that. True, the sceptic is one who accepts nothing based on trust and needs to investigate for themselves; but when convinced of a truth, they become an almost dogmatic convert. So the more appropriate name for this Arrow is that of the Enquirer. These people display scepticism as initial negativity to anything new, but once they investigate and prove it for themselves, their scepticism turns to avid acceptance. If they disagree with the new concept, they discard it forever.

The nature of these people is to investigate, thus many scientists have this Arrow. Generally, these people commence their investigations from the platform of basic orthodoxy, which is where they feel most comfortable in whatever discipline they follow. This does not imply they are heartless or unloving. Indeed, quite the reverse is true, for they have a keen sense of fairness and justice. However, their ability to grasp the deeper philosophical aspects of human life is often neglected, or relegated to a place of minor importance.

Uncertainties about life can easily arise if too much scepticism dominates their thinking, and so they become reactive. These people then become victims of the worry syndrome, which in turn often induces headaches and other nerve problems (sometimes affecting the eyes and ears). Worry and anxiety can cause unexpected reactions and lead to accidents that regularly involve the head. A sound philosophic understanding of life should be developed to help these people realise that there is far more in life than can be recognised through our five physical senses alone.

If orthodox religion, science or politics have, for any reason, proven disappointing or inadequate for these people, they tend to react by cultivating an agnostic outlook. This only leads to a deepening disenchantment with life. This is best combated by developing a sense of purpose, adopting stronger compassion toward all living things and enhancing the deeper aspects of their self-expression through writing, art, music, and so on.

○ *Children:* with this Arrow most frequently express their scepticism through moodiness. But once the parents understand its cause, they will be able to channel it into positive expression to help their children find inner peace, insulating them from rowdy television shows or noisy friends. When anything upsets these children, they turn inward. Their isolation is a means for them to recover mental and emotional balance.

The most positive help the parents can give is two-fold. First, encourage these children to read books on nature, science and geography, investigate the reasons behind things and develop a healthy curiosity. Second, encourage them to become active in an artistic pursuit, such as learning a musical instrument, painting, pottery and soon. Remember, these children need ample love and kindness, but not over-indulgence. Be patient but firm else children with this Arrow will readily take advantage. Parents should never withdraw their love from the child because it has not acted suitably. Remember, the child will invariably react to the parents, so the withdrawal of affection may encourage the child to "get even" in the only way it seems to know, by being spiteful or aloof. Love conquers all.

ARROW OF THE INTELLECT   *Birth date: 3/7/1960*

```
   3   6   9   ➤
   ────┼────┼────
   1        7
```

The presence of all three numbers on the Mind Plane indicates the importance of intellect and the dominance of mental activity in how people with this Arrow choose to express themselves. An extremely active brain is clearly indicated here, one in which the memory would be expected to dominate. Yet some people will be found to have a below-average memory in spite of being born with the Arrow of the Intellect. This clearly indicates that they have woefully wasted their talents and become mentally lazy. If not corrected, this will lead to the development of its destructive nature and ultimately loneliness as they lose friends because of their grumpiness.

Usually, people with this Arrow are bright, happy and alert, expressing preferences for things intellectual rather than aesthetic. They dwell far more in thought than feeling, though they can be quite emotional without actually realising it. They must avoid the tendency to develop an intellectual snobbishness by seeking only the company of those whom they consider to have a matching intellect or better. Developing tolerance and compassion will help them to master their tendency to display irritability towards those less blessed. Humans can overcome any deficiencies, so long as we wisely apply our natural talents.

Life brings more responsibility to these people than most, but they generally handle their obligations well and are happiest when performing duties for others. They are gregarious people who are rarely lost for words or rational explanations; but they need to watch the tendency to drive their brains too much without adequate rest. When this happens, they become inexplicably irritable. This is a warning to teach them that they must learn to balance their lives between the mental, artistic and physical to achieve optimum success. Yet, as simple as this seems, they sometimes find it a difficult concept to grasp, especially if they are not using their intuition. (It is important to remember that intuition is a function of the Soul Plane, not the mind – which is intellect.)

○ *Children:* with this Arrow frequently feature among the top in their classes at school, especially in mathematics and the analytical sciences. They should be graded as exceptional students and granted specialised tutorial care with the inclusion of such absorbing projects as research and astronomical investigations. These children are inclined to be restive and headstrong, especially when their active brains are not sufficiently inspired. They respond well when called upon for assistance and deeply appreciate praise for their efforts.

Take care that the diets of these children do not include stimulating foods or artificial chemicals. They are normally excitable youngsters and could easily laspe into mental hyperactivity with junk foods. A further problem occurs when their brains are working faster than their mouths, for they then tend to stutter, a habit that should be corrected as soon as it becomes apparent, best done by teaching them to relax more, play more sports, spend time in nature and "get out of their brains" for a while.

Always remember that children with this Arrow of the Intellect are constantly analysing, evaluating and assessing. They can easily tell when people are being less open and honest with them, or when they are being blatantly deceived. They react by withdrawing all confidence in the person. If such deception occurs often, these children can become very angry themselves.

ARROW OF POOR MEMORY   Birth date: 8/15/2007

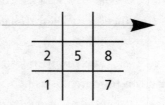

2	5	8
1		7

Absence of the numbers on the Mind Plane immediately implies a poor memory, but it does not mean that the person can't think or does not have a mind. Rather, the Arrow of Poor Memory tells us that the person has to work hard to keep their memory active, and they must continue to use their memory constantly throughout their lives. Once they become mentally lazy for a time, their memory, with its associated creativity and idealism, will rapidly lose its keenness. Severe problems often do not occur until mid-life, leading to a depletion of mental acuity. This commences gradually, develops into symptoms of childishness, then rapidly deteriorates into dementia, advanced cases of which are now known as Alzheimer's Disease.

Yet there are notable exceptions of people in past centuries who have mastered this handicap to successfully learn their primary lesson in life. To do so, they have been extremely diligent in their battle against slow learning and have had to maintain a constant mental alertness throughout their lives to keep them in top shape. These people will appear quite bright and witty, and their lives provide valuable lessons to the aware observer of life who will notice that significant handicaps can be successfully overcome.

○ **Children** with this Arrow will need special, patient training in their formative years. They will appear intellectually slow during infancy and must be trained to develop the power of concentration, vital for memory development. The expansion of their creative faculties through the arts and a sensitive awareness of nature, will also greatly help the Mind Plane to function.

These children should not start school until age five, possibly even as late as six, and then only to develop an awareness of discipline and learn about creative outlets. Their academic training should not commence until they reach at least the age of seven. If their scholastic pace is forced, they will invariably suffer headaches, perhaps leading to migraine. Remember, these children are far more interested in nature than they are in science, so they should be trained academically with care and patience, with due regard for their comparative slowness.

ARROW OF EMOTIONAL BALANCE   *Birth date: 5/23/1980*

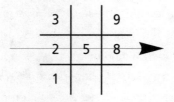

Of the three Planes, perhaps none reveals greater diversity of expression than the Soul Plane. As this is also the Feeling Plane, it governs the expression of emotions, our responses to life and the dominant way in which we relate to other people. People with this Arrow will show an endless variety of mannerisms.

These people possess a natural balance in their emotional life and a depth of spiritual understanding that can be especially beneficial in this emerging New Age of awareness. For these people, life is perceived as a balanced union of the physical and the spiritual, the former temporary and the latter permanent. It is this intensity of awareness that underlies their attitudes and tends to underscore their basic seriousness.

They should seek bright, happy company and the occasional pleasures of light entertainment to guard against becoming overly serious and withdrawn. They understand balance in spiritual terms, but tend to overlook its wider expression, embracing as it does the three Planes. Many take to the arts and entertainment fields to satisfy their deep love of balanced emotional expression, but must take care that they do not become too identified with the image they have created (or has been skilfully created for them). To maintain emotional balance, they need to be constantly aware of who is in charge of their emotions and never allow the emotions themselves to take control, or they will become lost and confused.

With such potentially powerful emotional control at their disposal, these people can become excellent actors. Their natural sensitivity allows them to thoroughly identify with their roles without sacrificing their precious individuality. People with this Arrow, whether actors or not, will play many different emotional roles in their daily activities, at work, socially and in the home.

The balanced sensitivity of people with this Arrow helps them to readily perceive other people's needs and attitudes. This can be put to excellent use in counselling and healing work for they have natural talents in these areas. As such, they should be properly trained in the healing arts and sciences with care to avoid dogmatism: no one discipline has the exclusive franchise on health care. Not only people with this Arrow, but all who enter the healing professions should be encouraged to maintain an open-minded approach. Over and above every other aspect, people with the Arrow of Emotional Balance need to realise that they have a feeling, sensitive nature and highly developed intuitive skill.

○ *Children* with this strong spiritual power can be so absorbed in their world of impressions that they are often regarded as dreamers.

They are especially susceptible to emotional conflicts, preferring to withdraw than become involved. Their desire to avoid disharmony can cause them to lag behind in their schooling and can impair their health if they allow their sensitivity to incite them to become reactive. Parents should be aware of the need for balanced emotional training for these children, a requirement that might well impose upon the parents the need to develop their own emotional control if it is not as it should be. It is highly advisable that such impressionable children avoid noisy or emotionally stimulating television or movies. They would also be best raised on a diet based on wholesome, natural foods, rather than pack-aged fast food with its stimulating chemical ingredients.

ARROW OF HYPERSENSITIVITY   *Birth date: 6/1/1971*

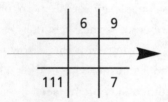

In contrast to the previous Arrow, when no numbers appear on the Soul Plane of the Birth Chart, varying degrees of emotional problems arise because of the emotional sensitivity of the person. Absence of these numbers does not imply that the person has no soul, rather that their soul protection is not strong and so their sen-sitivity is exposed to the outside world that often cruelly takes advantage of just such weakness.

These people are easily hurt, especially in their younger years before they learn to mask their feelings. They can be so easily offended or upset that they turn inward and become exceedingly shy. For many, this creates an early inferiority complex, causing them some difficulty when it comes to social contact and a loss of trust in other people. Most people outgrow this with maturity, learning to overcome it by taking control of their emotions, achieving fame in some recognised field of endeavour or manipulating conversations and situations to protect their sensitive natures. They sometimes develop the strategy of attack as their best line of defence, this being especially effective if they possess the Arrow of Intellect or a mind Ruling Number (see Chapter 7).

Their natural sensitivity gives them a deeply loving and tender nature, but they often become reactive due to intense personal hurt, causing them to develop an outer hardness that seems to be in conflict with their relaxed, natural expression. They learn to be quite discriminatory when it comes to showing their feelings, causing many with this Arrow to experience disappointment with their love life because they unwittingly misrepresent themselves.

Sometimes these people appear stubborn, other times bold (as a cover up of their inherent shyness), but always they have an emotional vulnerability that few with this Arrow really understand or master. Yet, emotional control is one of the most important lessons in life and must ultimately be embraced by all people, especially those with this Arrow of Hypersensitivity.

People who seek to overcome their hypersensitivity must first recognise the difference between reaction and positive action. They must cease to be the victim of circumstance or react to the opinions of others. Instead, let them learn to become the initiators, the inspirers of worthy endeavours. In this way, they will learn to recognise their strengths and use these to balance their personality and to achieve some measure of success in life. This provides a worthy basis for accomplishment, recognition and appreciation. As a consequence, their understanding will develop and their faith and confidence in humanity will be restored.

○ *Children* with this Arrow are exceptionally shy and sensitive, often recognised through mannerisms such as holding their head down in public. Yet, with patience, love and kindness, they can be easily guided to overcome this limitation. Parents need to take the time to listen to these children, for their fears, anxieties and concerns are very real to their immature minds. Encouraging these children to verbalise their problems is a very positive step in helping them develop balanced emotions and the feeling of safety to express their sensitivity.

Children with this Arrow of Hypersensitivity crave love, even more than most others, seeking every opportunity to serve those upon whom their love is centred. So parents should always endeavour to include these children in interesting activities, and when they do a good job, make certain to show them approval and appreciation, for that is their manna from heaven. If these children do a job poorly or appear to be disruptive or defiant, ensure that they are never scolded or criticised in the presence of other people, especially their peers. This is a certain way to entrench an inferiority complex and to lose their trust and respect. Instead, take them into a separate space and discuss the problem with them, helping them to find out how it can best be overcome.

ARROW OF PRACTICALITY ○ *Birth date: 4/23/1987*

3		9
2		8
1	4	7

These are the doing people of the world. With all numbers present on the Physical Plane, these people are only satisfied when they are involved in the practicalities of life. They are usually clever with their hands, but need direction to use their talents wisely, for they often decide to do things without thinking them through. However, their role is a primary one in human life – that of acquiring experience through involvement.

Their materialism will be intensified if people with this Arrow also possess a Ruling Number of 4, 7 or 10 (see Chapter 7). If their Ruling Number is of the Soul Plane, 2, 5, 8 or 11 (and in some cases 22/4), they will easily rise above material limitations and could become capable artists or musicians. Though they are generally motivated by kindness and the desire to help others, their heavy emphasis on the Physical Plane makes them poor judges of character.

Often these people are motivated by worldly desires and material ambition, unless they are intensely involved in creative work. Care should be taken to make sure they do not become too caught up in materialism, rather that they learn to utilise their power in a constructive way, either as a skilled tradesperson or as a practical organiser. If they become too materialistic, they could develop a harshness and cruelty whereby they are always seeking to be in control and never trust anybody to do as good as job as they think they can themselves. This earns them a begrudging respect only as and when they become powerful figures; but so far as their personality is concerned, much is left wanting.

It is vital that people with this Arrow of Practicality be taught to develop a balanced outlook from early in their lives. To acknowledge their sensitivity and understand other people's needs will greatly help them to find more happiness and fulfilment themselves.

○ *Children* with this Arrow exhibit a strong desire for material things from a very early age. Yet they are much happier in nature and when learning to appreciate the higher qualities of life. They are apt to take much for granted, so the virtue of appreciation and the value of sharing should be taught to them as soon as they are old enough to talk.

These children have decided likes and dislikes and should never be forced into doing anything to which they strongly object. Kindness and appreciation will always win the day with them, but never attempt to bribe them with money or gifts. Remember, they are physically motivated youngsters, so will rarely object to performing physical tasks, so long as they are appreciated. Yet, forcing them to do anything to which they have a strong objection will arouse resentment in them, leading to obstinacy. In turn, this could lead to destructiveness which, unless recognised and reversed, is likely to accentuate as they mature, leading to a possible criminal mentality in adulthood.

It is wise to keep them apart from children with known disruptive or destructive natures. Better they befriend the more sensitive and or thoughtful children to allow the balance to become apparent to them. They enjoy sharing things, so it would be useful to give them things that they can share. This will help them to develop their sensitivity of other people's needs.

ARROW OF DISORDER *Birth date: 2/2/2002*

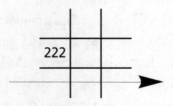

The purpose of incarnating on Earth is to give the soul the opportunity to further its evolvement toward perfection, using the vibrations that present themselves on Earth as the means for growth. Thus, to be born without any numbers on the Physical Plane is to accept a rather significant handicap that must be overcome if these people are to achieve any measure of happiness in their lives.

To have strengths on the Soul Plane or on the Soul and the Mind Planes alone is to lapse into a life of theory. Every feeling and every thought is theoretical until is it put into action through the Physical Plane and without physical action, life becomes extremely disordered and unfulfilled, depriving the person of some of the greatest gratification possible in human life, to witness our ideas successfully materialise. This is colloquially called "getting our act together."

Patient, practical experience in developing a balance over all the planes of expression is vital to people with the Arrow of Disorder, unless they intend living their lives in complete disorder. As they expand their sensitivity into practical expression, they will gradually develop an enjoyment such as can only manifest when tangible results are allowed to develop. Without this occurring, these people would become a drag on themselves and on society, for they would depend on government handouts and other charities for survival.

○ *Children* with this Arrow need to be taught to be practical and tidy from as early as when they can walk. They should be encouraged to do one thing at a time and to finish it before going on to the next. They will need considerable attention from their parents, who should make the time to play practical games with them, and get them to help in the garden and around the house. And for their successful efforts they should be rewarded with more than verbal appreciation. Though this is important, the need to see practical evidence is more so to help them develop an appreciation for balanced materialism. They should also be encouraged to take part in non-competitive sports and exercises from when they are old enough to go to school.

ARROW OF THE PLANNER   *Birth date: 3/12/1991*

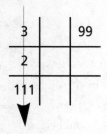

This is one of the most commonly found Arrows in both the 20th and 21st centuries. Due to the myriad occasions on which the numbers 1, 2 and 3 occur together in birth dates, it is little wonder that the world has been abundant in planners for so long. Joining, as it does, the gateway numbers on each of the three Planes, this Arrow links the ego's expression to the intuition of 2 to the memory and analytical qualities of 3. This gives rise to many inspired plans.

An inherent love of order, method and understanding is present here. However, it is usual that these planners prefer to concern themselves more with the function of organising than with the practical details (unless they also have the Arrow of Practicality on their Birth Charts or a practical Ruling Number of 4, 7, 10 or 22/4).

With such excellent capacities as planners, these people need to guard against subtle laziness. This has the tendency to develop when they perpetually derive plans for other people to enact without giving enough attention to the detail or the mode of operation of the plans as they are being executed. They often need to pay more attention to the smaller details and not succumb to the tendency of thinking them unimportant.

○ **Children** with this Arrow are happiest when organising some little plan of their own for their friends or parents. But when this runs counter to any plans of the parents, it could bring disappointments that only love and patience from the parents will help them to understand.

These children are inclined to be detached and take much for granted, so involved are they in their own thoughts and schemes. This detachment leads to aloofness, which often results in ignorance of other people's needs. Loving but firm discipline is needed to teach them the need for cooperation. They should never be bullied or threatened, instead they should be gently taught to respect the ideas, possessions and habits of others.

Such children have a trusting, gentle nature and are often slow to realise when injustices are perpetrated upon them. This naivety can be quite charming, though their gullibility can result in many hurts until they realise not everyone is as guileless as they are.

There is sometimes a nervous restlessness in their earlier years, resulting from the inclination to spend too much time in their mind without knowing quite how to translate this mental energy into the physical. Encouragement to become physically active and to get out into nature will help considerably. Reading illustrated travel books will also be of benefit until they have the means of undertaking the travel themselves, for this satisfies their love of investigating and exploring the unknown.

ARROW OF THE WILL   Birth date: 4/26/1952

6	9
22	5	
1	4	

When the creative number 6 links to the freedom to express itself (5) then to the number of organisation (4), we have a powerful balance of the three centre numbers of each Plane. This is called the Arrow of the Will. It symbolises the human spine and the life force that flows through it.

During the period from 1889 to 1999, everyone born with the Arrow of Will also has the Arrow of Determination, which makes for very dynamic people. Even so, we find not too many famous people with this combination, due to a tendency to forcefully assert their power by overriding the feelings and wishes of others. So powerful is their driving force that they frequently ignore advice from others and rarely take heed of their own intuition.

The special power of this Arrow lies in its integration and balance of the strengths of each Plane. When people recognise the power of that balance and apply it to their daily affairs, their lives transform and they experience optimum success. They have the fortitude and courage to brook all odds when they act with wisdom, such as we have historically seen from the lives and brilliant works of the two most famous bearers of this Arrow, William Shakespeare and Leonardo da Vinci.

○ *Children* with this Arrow can be a handful. They are exceptionally strong-willed, but must be trained to understand other people's points of view and accept wise guidance when it is offered. One of their greatest pleasures comes from doing kind deeds, but they need to be guided to take care not to impose ulterior motives of self-interest when undertaking such deeds.

Unless these children are guided with patience and love, they can become exceedingly stubborn and quite obnoxious. They respond very readily to appreciation expressed as loving praise, but become instantly suspicious if offered material tokens such as sweets or money. If they were to accept such gifts, it would induce a mercenary nature that could result in a hard materialist attitude as they mature.

ARROW OF FRUSTRATION *Birth date: 12.21.1973*

3	↑	9
22		
111		7

With the absence of numbers 4, 5 and 6, this Arrow reveals a divided Birth Chart and, all too often, a weak will. In the post-war years of the 1940s, 1950s and 1960s, birth dates with this Arrow did not occur. But since the beginning of 1970, we find many people with the Arrow of Frustration. As practitioners we especially come across many with this Arrow, for they are often the sufferers of broken homes, unhappy relationships and intense personal confusion.

Frustration has to be known for what it really is, unfulfilled expectation. These people often expect more from others than they themselves are prepared to give. Yet if only they would learn to see people for who and what they are and to appreciate them for their own uniqueness, such expectations would not be misplaced. The habit of expecting is an emotionally-driven demand. Far better that we replace it with "preference" to allow us to accept what eventuates, recognising it as the best for all concerned. Then we do not have an emotional demand tied to the outcome of the event. This allows other people to be themselves, instead of reacting to what we might expect of them.

We need to realise that no one is everything they could be. If they were, they would not have needed this incarnation. We are all at various stages of personal growth and it should never be forced, any more than a rose bud should be forced to open prematurely. For humans, appreciation is the best growth stimulant, but it must be genuine to be of lasting value.

Life has many different ways of ensuring that its lessons are learned. People with the Arrow of Frustration are aware that the losses, separations and disillusionments that life presents (and there can be quite a few), are vital steps in a long process of evolving toward perfection. As they develop in awareness, their disappointments in others will diminish and eventually disappear as they mature in wisdom. If not, they take on the mantle of sadness, loneliness and dejection. As they develop compassion, they will become happier, finding that their earlier frustration was little more than a carry-over from a less than happy childhood.

○ *Children* with this Arrow need a special depth of love and attention. Life to them can become unfairly victimising as they experience acute disappointments in friends and even in casual acquaintances who let them down. This creates moodiness, dejection most particularly, which confuses and upsets them.

Parents must teach these children to be prepared to allow others to be themselves, and to know that other people will not always do what they want when they want it. In this way, they learn to "prefer" rather than "expect" so they are not emotionally hooked to the outcomes. Feeling a strong bond of friendship with their parents is important for these children. This is much more than respect and obedience, it is loving trust. Such special friendship will minimise the child's moodiness, especially if they know they can talk openly with their parents and not be harshly judged or called upon to explain or justify themselves.

ARROW OF ACTIVITY Birth date: 7/8/1989

```
        |     |    ▲
        |     |   99
  ------+-----+------
        |     |   88
  ------+-----+------
        |     |
    1   |     |    7
```

Many more people in the 20th century will be found to have this Arrow than will be the case in the 21st century. It is the Arrow of great expression: the experience number (7) links to the number of wisdom and perceptiveness (8) then to the ambitiousness and responsibility of 9. Such forcefulness as is available from this combination can produce more than balanced activity, it can be taken overboard into hyperactivity.

Humans are by nature the most expressive of creatures, so diverse is their range of expression, far beyond that of any other living form. Such natural expressiveness is concentrated to a more than average degree when a person has this Arrow. Yet, constraints of modern society tend to inhibit freedom of expression to the extent that people with this Arrow can easily become agitated by the accumulation of suppressed nervous energy. The result is often extreme nervousness that might induce any number of ailments, including asthma, digestive upsets, headaches, migraines, or heart or circulatory problems.

Peace and harmony are necessary for these people. Arguments, rowdy radios or televisions, and so on, will become particularly distressing for them, inducing stress-related illness. They need to spend as much time as possible in nature, for they are not happy city dwellers. Bushwalks, farming, gardening and most open air sports are ideal for these people. Without such freedom, their digestive systems will often rebel, a condition exacerbated by a poor diet. A healthy diet and time spent in nature, together with a positive outlook on life and happy friends, will keep people with the Arrow of Activity healthier than any medicine.

○ *Children* with this Arrow are especially susceptible to high levels of noise, demanding peace, love and harmony in all they do and wherever they go. Being highly excitable and impressionable, they need the freedom of the outdoors and to be in nature as much as possible. They are happiest when allowed to sleep, eat and play outdoors, for then their emotions are less taxed. They need plenty of sleep, and a home that is free of disharmony and tension.

Noisy or disturbed conditions can cause serious setbacks to the schooling of these children, as well as impeding their social adjustments. Their great need is for peace, anything short of this will interfere with their mental and emotional dispositions. They should be protected from noisy or violent television or films, otherwise their nerves will suffer. In fact, any violent or unnatural surroundings will be potentially upsetting to them. This fact is especially pertinent to newborn babies with this Arrow.

From the early 1970s, the dramatic increase in Sudden Infant Death Syndrome (SIDS) has rung alarm bells throughout the medical profession. A vast amount of money has been raised to investigate this "mysterious death." However, the solution is simple, the problem neither a disease nor mysterious. The newly born infant with this Arrow of Activity is in dire need of peace and natural surroundings. Yet when it is born into an air-conditioned hospital ward, spanked to induce crying and kept separate from the only source of support it has known for nine months, it is hardly surprising that it has so much trouble integrating itself into such a new and seemingly hostile environment. Many just do not make it, preferring to re-cast their karmic lot for a future body that might be more conducive to their evolutionary needs. (The other major factor is biochemical, where the mother has a lowered immune system from smoking, alcohol or drugs, and the weakened immunity of the infant is unable to cope with both problems simultaneously.)

ARROW OF PASSIVITY   *Birth date:* 1/1/2000

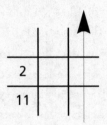

People with this Arrow will be the thinkers, planners and behind-the-scenes guides of the new millennium, but they will certainly not be the achievers unless they undertake a tremendous amount of intense training in perseverance.

With the qualities such as these people represent, the world will see less war and human turmoil than it has in the past few centuries when its opposite, the Arrow of Activity, was more often present. Passivity is not the opposite of activity as far as human expression is concerned, rather it suggests a natural desire to live a balanced, harmonious life where peaceful coexistence prevails. This is a potential boon for the 21st century.

The negative aspect of this Arrow will need to be recognised and guarded against. It will manifest as laziness and inertness people with this Arrow failing to recognise that their purpose in life is to learn through experience. They will need to be taught to be more physically active in their daily routines. The earlier in life these activities commence, the easier it will become for them to develop useful habits.

○ *Children* with this Arrow will also need to be encouraged toward greater physical involvement in their daily life. This will be best done by example their parents using loving encouragement to get their children to participate in sports and exercise. Spending significant time outdoors in nature will also be greatly beneficial to these children.

BIRTH CHARTS WITH NO ARROWS

Occasionally, we see Birth Charts that have neither Arrows of strength nor of weakness, such as when a person is born on 7/12/1960.

	6	9
2		
11		7

The lack of Arrows does not signify any special attribute other than to indicate that the person needs to devote more time and perseverance to the development of their strengths than might have otherwise been. They are generally quite adaptable people who find it easy to fit into most social and vocational situations. The primary lesson they need to develop is that of wise assertiveness.

○ *Children* with no Arrows are rather easy going and generally quite happy in life. However, they should not be taken for granted. Rather, they should be encouraged with loving care to do things that they enjoy, which will help them to become more assertive about things that are of special importance to them.

CHAPTER .07

The Ruling Numbers

"EVOLUTION IS THE LAW OF LIFE
NUMBER IS THE LAW OF THE UNIVERSE
UNITY IS THE LAW OF GOD."

— Pythagoras as quoted by Edouard Schure
in his book *The Great Initiates*

*A*t varying speeds, we are all travellers on the Path. Some have stopped and are resting, indeed too many have rested for too long. Some are making discursive tours on tracks that lead away from the Path, tracks that appear to offer many a rich inducement, yet dissipate into nothing more than a confirmation that we have only one primary Path. And this we must transit before further growth can be successfully undertaken.

To pass through this life without at least fulfilling our primary goals is like entering a golf tournament with only a putter. Such frustration invariably results from lack of guidance or self-discovery. Yet so many people are led onto paths where their talents are not fully utilised and satisfaction is anything but complete, while others drift into jobs or activities that are as far removed from their most suitable pathways as bricklaying is for a ballerina.

If senior school students were to be taught to know their Ruling Numbers, their search for a suitable vocation after leaving school would be far more rewarding. They would be guided to a suitable job or to advanced study appropriate to their nature, rather than scouring the diverse job market to half-heartedly accept whatever came their way. Thousands of existing unemployed people would be happily engaged in work, were they but familiar with their most suitable vocations as indicated by their Ruling Numbers.

Fortunately, more and more people are realising that to discover and follow their Path is the most rewarding thing they can do in life. Once we have found it only a fool would depart from it. We know that to choose any alternative is to accept a shabby deal and that is not what life has in store for us.

As we seek to unite with the Creator, we shed, one by one, the cloaks of imagery we have dressed in, and that represent how we choose to appear in the world. As they fall away, the growth of our real personality emerges, revealing the beautiful psyche, the core of our personal universe, our raison d'être, as the French so eloquently put it. We no longer seek excuses, blame others or deny our personal responsibility.

This personal evolution is our progress along the Path. And our Path is, as a matter of course, in total harmony with the law of the Universe. But remember that our Path is a neverending journey along the infinite road toward perfection, and our Ruling Number is that vital primary pathway through which we must evolve before we undertake further progress in life. Some people never evolve beyond their Ruling Number, yet if they have secured the lessons of their Ruling Number in one lifetime, at least they have made progress. Others are not content with such constraints, recognising the emerging potential for growth, excitement and joy that inspires their life as they evolve beyond the agenda of their primary pathway, their natal Ruling Number.

Before a tree can bear fruit, it must grow in strength and maturity. So it is with human life. Our strength and maturity emerge as we fulfil our primary purpose in life, as simply revealed by our Ruling Number.

Our Ruling Number is found by first adding each individual number in our birth date together. We then add those numbers together until we get (in most cases bar three) a single digit number. For example, if we take the birth date January 3, 1960 and rewrite it numerically as 1/3/1960, we get 20 as a result if we add all the numbers together: $1 + 3 + 1 + 9 + 60 = 20$. This total is then reduced to a single digit number by simple adding $2 + 0$, which of course is 2. So, the Ruling Number of a person born on January 3, 1960 is shown as 1/3/1960 = 20/2.

To clearly illustrate how each Ruling Number (11 in total) is obtained, the following birth dates have been used as examples:

- MAY 1 1940: 5/1/1940 = 20/2 – RULING NUMBER OF 2
- MAY 2 1940: 5/2/1940 = 21/3 – RULING NUMBER OF 3
- MAY 3 1949: 5/3/1949 = 31/4 – RULING NUMBER OF 4
- MAY 4 1949: 5/4/1949 = 32/5 – RULING NUMBER OF 5
- MAY 5 1949: 5/5/1949 = 33/6 – RULING NUMBER OF 6
- MAY 6 1949: 5/6/1949 = 34/7 – RULING NUMBER OF 7
- MAY 7 1949: 5/7/1949 = 35/8 – RULING NUMBER OF 8
- MAY 8 1949: 5/8/1949 = 36/9 – RULING NUMBER OF 9
- MAY 9 1949: 5/9/1949 = 37/10 – RULING NUMBER OF 10
- MAY 1 1949: 5/1/1949 = 29/11 – RULING NUMBER OF 11
- MAY 3 1940: 5/3/1940 = 22/4 – RULING NUMBER OF 22/4

Note that in Pythagorean numerology there is no Ruling Number 1. Some other systems tend to use the Ruling 1, oblivious to the fact that it is the only absolute number, all other numbers being relative to it and incorporating it. In the sixth century BC, Pythagoras recognised 1 as the number symbolising unity in the world and ego in humans. Thus, as every number contains the 1, in Pythagorean numerology we find the Ruling Number 10 instead of a Ruling Number 1. Therefore, birth dates totalling 19, 28, 37 or 46 become Ruling Number 10s.

The Ruling Number 10 is the first of the three compounded Ruling Numbers. The other two are Ruling Number 11 and Ruling Number 22/4. These two have a special metaphysical significance: the 11 is the highest spiritual number and the 22/4 (twenty-two four) is the double 11 underpinned by the practical 4, combining to form a truly masterful combination.

The 22 is recognised for its special significance in many metaphysical and scientific systems. It represents the highest card in the Major Arcana of the tarot. In basic mathematics, the 22 represents the circle, for it is the lowest whole number to which the ratio of the circumference with the diameter of a circle relates – 22:7, symbolised as $\prod$ (Pi).

Metaphysically, the circle represents eternal life, having neither beginning nor end. Mathematically, the circle is zero (representing nothing if it is the numerator of a fraction), or infinity (if it is the denominator of a fraction).

Clearly, a master number must have unique numerological symbolism – 22 does, 33 does not. Some numerologists have ascribed to the Ruling Number 33/6 the epithet of "master number." In so doing, they have grossly overlooked the very foundation of Pythagorean numerology – that mathematical logic and spiritual reason exist behind every facet of the study. So let us not waste time on numerological aberrations; the Ruling Number 33/6 is a powerful mind number that combines strong imagination with creativity, but it is NOT a master number.

In providing the following analyses of the Ruling Numbers, I have formulated my research on the ancient teachings of Pythagoras, and have expanded them to meet the needs of modern society, based on over 40 years of personal study, research and practice.

○ RULING NUMBER 2

Only one total of numbers in the birth date will result in a Ruling Number 2, that is the total of 20. (Totals of 29, 38 and 47 result in Ruling Number 11s.) Therefore, we find far fewer people with a Ruling 2 (and Ruling 22/4) than any other of the Ruling Numbers. Not surprisingly, both Ruling Numbers suggest a special significance. The Ruling 2 is generally the sensitive, unassuming, supportive person, while the Ruling 22/4 is far more assertive and self-confident.

○ *Life's purpose*

These people have a special ability to work with and under the guidance of dynamic leadership. Without this, they could feel lost. They are generally not leaders themselves, rarely possessing the desire to lead, yet they do have a unique ability to seek and associate with the type of person or organisation with which their diligent capabilities may be most appreciated. Their special role is to complement by providing loyal, intuitive support.

○ *Best expression*

Though extremely capable and confident when allowed to work at their own steady pace, Ruling 2s can be made to feel insecure if burdened with stress and persistent urgency. They must be allowed to progress at their own natural pace for they prefer to consolidate as they go. They are exceptionally honourable and dislike their integrity being doubted – this would also undermine their confidence. Their best expression is generally through the sensitive use of their hands, such as in art or in writing, but always when guided by their faithful intuition.

○ *Distinctive traits*

They are intuitive, sensitive, reliable, diligent and compassionate people. They are the peacemakers, sometimes to the extent of reforming (and in the current emerging age of awareness, this is a very valuable ability). Ruling 2s are less motivated by ego than are most people, exhibiting the selfless and noble acumen of being able to merge their ego with that of others when desirable or necessary.

○ *Negative tendencies to be surmounted*

Some Ruling 2s fail to realise that their inherent development must result from personal involvement. Materialism or a false sense of egocentricity will impel them to become discontented, irritable and frustrated. But these characteristics are both rare and unnatural to them. In the event of such a situation occurring, they will eventually recognise the departure from their path of natural development. Another area of disappointment derives from relying too much on rationalisation at the expense of their intuition, for this will lead to errors in judgement.

○ *Recommended development*

Ruling 2s should employ their powerful intuitive ability to develop self-confidence and to choose as friends and associates those who accept and appreciate their distinctive traits. This is important for their personal development. As they mature, Ruling 2s naturally discover the importance of emotional control, learning how to use it as an aid to their sensitive expression. It will be of considerable benefit to them to develop their mental faculties, especially their powers of deduction and memory. Such development will firmly anchor their self-esteem and provide greater personal happiness.

○ *Most suitable vocations*

These people are best suited to work as personal assistants to administrators, especially in charitable or educational activities. They are also artistic, with a sensitivity that is capably expressed in painting, music, song or dance, but they feel more comfortable as part of a group, rather than a soloist. They are sometimes found as capable diplomats, social workers, secretaries and, if limited by lack of education, process workers.

○ *Summary*

Ruling 2s are sensitive, intuitive, supportive, reliable, peacemaking, compassionate and artistic.

○ *Notes for the 21st century*

The last Ruling 2 person to be born in the 20th century was on january 1, 1980. The first in the 21st century was born on 7/29/2000, thereafter many have and will be born. Thus the sensitive nature of the Ruling 2 will not be so unique, hopefully encouraging an increased movement toward intuitiveness and peace throughout the world.

○ *Famous Ruling 2's*

Prince Philip born June 10, 1921
Ronald Reagan born February 2, 1911

○ RULING NUMBER 3

When we note its commanding position at the head of the mind plane , we realise why so much emphasis is placed on thinking and on reasoning by people whose Ruling number is 3. These are people whose birth date numbers total 12, 21, 30, 39 or 48.

○ Life's purpose

As these people emphasise the thinking aspects of life, it is clear that their primary purpose relates to their mental capabilities. For them, the understanding of life and the development of their personality are significantly related to their thought processes in preference to intuitiveness or practical involvement. Their service to the community and their favoured mode of expression is therefore primarily expressed through thinking, planning, analysing, memorising, and so on.

○ Best expression

The speed with which Ruling 3 people engage in mental work often leaves others well behind. Their acute mental alertness is sometimes surprisingly expressed in a keen sense of humour, a natural wit that makes them bright and intelligent company and excellent hosts and hostesses. It should be remembered that they invariably express themselves far more fluently through the thinking channels than either emotionally or physically.

○ Distinctive traits

Their active brain, lively sense of humour and general mental alertness contribute to a successful working and social life for the Ruling 3s. They are often the life of the party or the brightest person in the office, but this success does not always prevail in their homes. While they express a natural wit for superficial contacts, with constant companions they often become overly critical. This can be very wearing on people who are close, especially on the spouse. Ruling 3s enjoy helping people, so long as they have the rapport on mental level and the other people are prepared to cooperate.

○ Negative tendencies to be surmounted

When not living constructively, these people often assume an unpleasant air or superiority. This can create many misunderstandings and lead to considerable unhappiness. Being so mentally alert, negative Ruling 3s readily show a lack of patience and an intolerance of others less blessed, becoming quite critical of their "limitations." This fault-finding is invariably carried into their homes, involving them in broken marriages. In some instances, the constant criticism can become such a heavy burden upon the spouse that it will lead to the spouse's shortened life span.

○ *Recommended development*

Ruling 3 people must learn to develop a sensitivity to the feelings of others. When they recognise that life's experiences provide a constant school of learning, their graduation rate is greatly improved. It is also greatly improved when they learn to live with others in harmony. This then makes for a more positive outlook on life.

they must not learn to blame others, but to use their natural power of resilience to bounce back with renewed vigour, looking upon an "unfavourable" experience as a helpful opportunity for growth. It will be of great benefit to them to broaden their means of expression by cultivating their intuitiveness and by being more practical in day-to-day affairs, especially around the home. For example, by actually mowing the lawn rather than theorising about how it should be done or employing a gardener.

○ *Most suitable vocations*

Ruling 3 people are best suited to work in those vocations that involve mental activity. This includes the academic fields, particularly the sciences, accountancy, business management, computer programming, system analysis, and so on. They can be excellent research scientists and will also excel in some of the arts, such as writing and acting in light entertainment, or as critics of the arts.

○ *Summary*

These people enjoy entertaining others, for they feel at home as the life of the party. Their minds are constantly alert and assessing, planning and thinking. They possess an intelligent sense of humour, yet often experience marriage problems.

○ *Famous Ruling 3's*

Bill Cosby born July 12, 1937
Fidel Castrol born August 13, 1926
Katherine Hepburn born November 9, 1909
Vivien Leigh born November 5, 1913

○ RULING NUMBER 4

In the modern world, where so much general emphasis is placed on material concerns, the basic expression of most people with a Ruling 4 can be easily gratified. But there is more to them than materialism, though their major emphasis certainly lies on the physical, the 4 located in the centre of the physical plane.

○ *Life's purpose*

While we continue to live on earth in a physical body, it is natural that so much of our experience is related to the material aspects of life. Ruling 4 people in particular emphasise physical experience and expression, which is vital to their early development. But as they mature, the natural tendency is for these people to embrace more of the organising aspect of the practical plane, thereby facilitating greater scope in their development of love, awareness and wisdom.

○ *Best expression*

Ruling 4 people have an extensive spectrum of expression, encompassing most physical work or work that involves organisation. It can range from the pleasure of making money as an end in itself, or to the challenges of establishing gigantic business deals, through to the practical aspects of art and cultural affairs or the involvement in sporting events. In whatever they do, Rulings 4s generally prefer the conventional approach to the experimental, being more orthodox than adventurous. In general, they are the doers of the world.

○ Distinctive traits

These are people with a natural flair for the practical – they generally prefer to do a thing rather than discuss its merits. Their love of practicality keeps Ruling 4 people on the go. They can rarely sit still and watch others do the organising, and invariably come forward and offer worthwhile assistance. They are among the most systematic, reliable and trustworthy people. This is especially evident in detailed work, where their accuracy and practical ability are often second to none. On matters of a practical nature, Ruling 4s can manifest extraordinary patience, but where intellectual or spiritual matters are concerned they are more impatient.

○ Negative tendencies to be surmounted

It is quite common for Ruling 4 people to become totally absorbed in their work and to unthinkingly neglect to bring balance to their lives, especially their home life. If they do not have a strong emotional equilibrium, they can easily lose heart due to frustrated ambition, leading to nerve problems and stress-induced illnesses. Should they neglect the need for a balanced life, an overly materialistic outlook could easily develop. This can lead to emotional insecurity and chronic unhappiness, greatly inhibiting the development of their purpose in life, namely practical service.

○ *Recommended development*

Three important avenues of development should be undertaken by Ruling 4s: relaxation, mental application and expanded intuitiveness. Relaxation is an important means of achieving detachment from material concerns and from physical involvements when both become excessive. It also provides an excellent basis for mental and spiritual growth. Such relaxation is best achieved through meditation. The most suitable forms of mental application lie in memory training and understanding underlying principles, such as are taught in philosophy, engineering, architecture, and so on. Such applications will give rise to an expanded intuitive awareness, the doorway to spiritual consciousness. In all their affairs, Ruling 4s should strive to balance their practicality with their mental (analytical, creative and idealistic) and their spiritual (intuitive, loving and wise) faculties.

○ *Most suitable vocations*

These people are best suited to work as skilled tradespeople, technicians, crafts people and machinists, as well as managers, professional sports people, economists, physicians, chiropractors and horticulturists – all depending on the level of education. In financial matters, they need to develop a heightened of judgement to ensure they are not motivated by personal avarice. Many teachers of manual arts, sports and fitness, as well as authors of technical books and magazines, are found among Ruling 4s.

○ **Summary**

Ruling 4s are practical and conventional in outlook, often materialistic. They are interested in sports and very capable with their hands. They are doing people.

○ *Famous Ruling 4's*

Arnold Schwarzenegger born july 30, 1947

Paul Hogan born 0ctober 8, 1939

Joseph Stalin born December 21, 1879

Yasser Arafat born February 17, 1929

Elton John born March 25, 1947

Michael Parkinson born March 28, 1935

Kerry Packer born December 17, 1937

Martina Navratilova born October 18, 1956

○ RULING NUMBER 5

In practice, we find that people with the Ruling number 5 invariably strive to be free from constriction. This is a natural expression of their highly sensitive nature and their inherent need to express their feelings. It is not surprising when we realise that 5 is the centre of the Soul Plane and of the Arrow of the Will. Birth dates whose component numbers total 14, 23, 32 or 41 have a Ruling Number 5.

○ *Life's purpose*

The mastery of sensitive expression (be it through writing, painting, sculpture, and so on) is one of the real refinements of human endeavour. However, it can only be achieved when adequate freedom prevails. It is just this type of expression that Ruling 5 people seek to develop as a means of acquiring the command and understanding of their emotions. But few of them are aware of this, feeling only the drive for freedom, ignorant of its real reason, which is to learn to constructively direct their lives by its means.

○ *Best expression*

Most of these people find it difficult to work to strictly regulated hours. For this, they invariably blame the boss and often suffer stress-related illnesses as a result. They should seek work that allows them to be free of immediate direction, such as that of a travelling salesperson, freelance writer or artist. In this way, they will enjoy a much-needed freedom to develop their most suitable avenue of expression. Many feel the strong desire for adventure and readily take to travel or frequent job changes (many of them become relegated to the dole line). Done with wisdom and awareness, travel and varied experience can be their most valuable means of attaining needed freedom and enlightenment. A further field in which Ruling 5s happily express their feelings is the entertainment field, and many eminently succeed as professional entertainers. But in whatever they do, their love of people is a primary motivation.

○ Distinctive traits

Ruling 5 people are intuitive, with deep feelings and a strong artistic flair, who gain immeasurable pleasure from being free to express themselves. With such freedom, they are lively and dynamic; but if confined, they tend to become sullen and moody, even apathetic. Yet they are usually very good-natured people with a strong determination to enjoy life and to help others do so as well – an aspect of their compassionate nature.

○ Negative tendencies to be surmounted

Such a strong love of freedom can sometimes drive Ruling 5 people to take employment in illegal activities to avoid being confined to an orthodox job. They thereby fail to recognise the purpose of such apparent confinement: to learn vital lessons in patience, cooperation and self-control. Many young Ruling 5s, taking their first job, rebel at having to answer to a boss and decide to take unemployment benefits. When inattentive to detail, Ruling 5s make poor business-people, a problem further exacerbated by their nervousness and uncertainty when confined to the workaday world. Their resultant irritability can become a precursor to stress and depression if not controlled. Care should be taken to restore calm by spending more time in nature.

○ *Recommended development*

Very often a person's search for freedom is a hankering for those pristine days of carefree innocence. Clearly we cannot live in history, save for the application of its lessons towards our further development. Thus, when current circumstances appear to con- strict us, we should be aware of the lessons we are intended to learn from them. Then we can move forward, graduating from such confinement, which so many Ruling 5s readily identify. Part of such graduating is the need for these people to develop increased attention to detail, thereby embracing a wider perspective to life afforded by greater practicality. They will find it to their benefit to accept suitable travel opportunities to develop their powers of observation as a vital means of understanding more about life and the development of wisdom. As they mature, their recognition of the importance of balanced discipline will strengthen their personal security, especially in the area of relationships. Above all, it must be remembered that Ruling 5 people are love motivated, irrespective of how they represent themselves to the world. Thus, they naturally respond to genuine appreciation and give it in return.

○ *Most suitable vocations*

Freedom, acting and art summarise the essential Ruling 5 expression. This qualifies them best for working as acting professionals (whether it be on the stage or behind the scenes, salespeople or as politicians); in the travel or hospitality industries; or as writers, artists, entrepre- neurs, designers, inventors, social workers or reformers.

○ *Summary*

Their nature is essentially loving and freedom-loving, artistic, adventurous and moody, oscillating between joviality when free to be emotionally expressive and sullenness when feeling suppressed. Essentially, they are "feeling" people.

○ *Famous Ruling 5's*

Abraham Lincoln born February 12, 1809
Greg Norman born February 10, 1955
Vincent Van Gogh born March 30, 1853
Irving Berlin born May 11, 1888
Adolf Hitler born April 20, 1889
Johnny Carson born October 23, 1925

○ RULING NUMBER 6

This is a Ruling number of extremes. These people have the potential for great creative power when living positively, yet they become incessant worriers when living negatively. The position of this number at the centre of the Mind Plane and at the head of the Arrow of Will gives Ruling 6 people tremendous potential to perceive and create brilliantly. Regrettably, they rarely achieve lasting success in their lives due to their ever-present tendency to worry (their self-destruction). Birth dates with component numbers totalling 15, 24, 33 or 42 have a Ruling Number 6.

○ *Life's purpose*

Here we find people who excel in a wide range of creative endeavours, from the home to the stage of world fame. This implies a very important responsibility in life, one that demands a deep, loving dedication. All people with the Ruling 6 have this natural capacity, but often they become so physically identified with their responsibilities that anxiety and worry entrap them in a web of stress. They must learn to master those situations into which their great capacity for care and creativity draw them, rather than let the situations control them. To this end, they must learn the art of loving detachment so that they may express their beautiful creativity without being imposed upon.

○ Best expression

These people excel in positions where their trust, creativity and deep sense of caring responsibility are called for. Some prefer to express these talents publicly, excelling on stage or screen with acting and or singing. Others choose to utilise their loving nature more privately in the home and with their family. At the core of their expression is always that deep love of humanity and a loving good nature that ever seeks expression and is always a joy to behold.

○ Distinctive traits

Their exceptional creativity finds every opportunity to express itself at work, at play and in the home. To Ruling 6 people, their home is the most important place; it occupies a considerable amount of their time and is second in importance only to their loved ones in it. Great humanitarians, these people resent injustices of any kind. They are exceptionally loving, unselfish and tolerant people who must guard against being imposed upon. Remember, this is a mind number, exerting significant influence on its bearer's attitudes.

○ Negative tendencies to be surmounted

When opportunities for expressing their creativity are limited to the home, overemphasis, sometimes to the point of fanaticism, can create unhealthy anxieties and an unbalanced possessiveness. This can lead to apprehensiveness, fear and or anxiety such that their personal growth is severely constricted and their life becomes stagnant. Worry often becomes so chronic it results in mild psychosis, bringing with it a sad loneliness that is totally in conflict with everything they were endeavouring to create. When worry and negativity prevail in the lives of Ruling 6s, they adopt a whining voice and take on the air of fault-finder.

○ *Recommended development*

Ruling 6 people must always realise that a positive mental outlook is of utmost importance in the development of creativity, whatever the physical limitations. They must come to realise that loving concern should never detract from one's freedom of expression. As such, they should avoid the tendency for possessiveness, instead channelling their abilities into expressing themselves creatively. Most Ruling 6 people have a desire for peace at any price, but such acquiescing can be construed as weakness, ultimately becoming self-destructive and leading to unhappiness. Developing a wise firmness will improve their happiness; it assists to guard them against being imposed upon by thoughtless people (and this can even include members of the family). Developing their ability to distinguish between the important and unimportant aspects of their life, embracing an acute sense of temperance and expressing their compassion wisely will all contribute to the more effective channelling of their powerful creative faculties, their ability to produce the unexpected.

○ *Most suitable vocations*

Whatever they do they must have creative prospects that are directly or ultimately designated for the betterment of human welfare. They excel in humanitarian organisations, and as healers, artists and designers. They have a remarkable ability for dramatic singing and acting, some even taking this to extremes by overdramatising their lives.

○ *Summary*

Ruling 6 people are creative, caring, just, unselfish, tolerant and home loving, but inclined toward deep worry and extreme anxiety.

○ *Famous Ruling 6's*

Agatha Christie born September 15, 1890
Sylvester Stallone born July 6, 1946
Meryl Streep born June 22, 1949
Charles De Gaulle born November 22, 1890
Jesse Jackson born October 8, 1941

○ RULING NUMBER 7

Under the influence of this Ruling Number, people gain maximum experience from life's lesson book, both through the personal sacrifice of learning and through teaching or sharing (teaching the consummate means of learning). Both facets of human growth are intimately related to physical expression, symbolised by the position of the 7 the birth chart at the intersection of the Arrows of Practicality and Activity. Birth dates with component numbers totalling 16, 25, 34 and 43 have a Ruling Number 7.

○ *Life's purpose*

It would appear that the manner in which individual human development takes place in life ensures that each soul incarnates with a Ruling Number 7 when it is necessary to undertake a major step forward. The unique aspect of this Ruling Number is its almost limitless capacity for learning through personal involvement. Enlightenment acquired in such a manner invariably qualifies Ruling 7 people to capably share their experiences, making them excellent teachers. And the practical realisations of their experiences equips them with a profound and abiding philosophy of life.

○ *Best expression*

One of the most important requirements for Ruling 7 people is that they are allowed to learn their way. They can accept little more than minimum direction from others, for they hunger to learn by personal involvement and expression. This involvement demands of them sacrifices in either one or more of those three aspects of human life that hit us most: health, love and or money. This qualifies them as very practical teachers and helpers of humankind. However, while they are not averse to implementing discipline in others, they find someone else's discipline very difficult to live with.

○ *Distinctive traits*

These people are found among the most active in life. Though not always conscious of it, their driving force is the profound need for personal experience and these experiences become the most memorable (unfortunately) when they imply some form of personal sacrifice. This is the path of the Ruling 7 person, many of whom appear to suffer rather sad lives, especially when they do not learn from their earlier experiences and repetitions induce harsher sacrifices. However, from the loss of health, love and or money, they acquire a deep philosophical understanding that ultimately assists them to avoid such harsh lessons as their conscious awareness develops. They possess a powerful, natural fortitude that often appears to provide them with an inherent self-confidence which, in turn, assists them to handle their life's experiences much more stoically than outsiders often realise. Their abiding philosophy is that everything occurs for a purpose.

○ *Negative tendencies to be surmounted*

Their compulsion for personal experience, to the extent of often rejecting guidance, can cause Ruling 7s to become extremely rebellious. In refusing to accept advice, they tend to adopt the attitude that they like to teach but they do not like to be taught. This can bring much sadness into their lives when they fail to learn from the experiences of others. Yet, they often seek to have other people follow their advice and become annoyed if they get the same advice as they give others. Until they mature and act with greater wisdom, their domestic and business lives will often be far from happy.

○ Recommended development

We often find that Ruling 7s are not the best judges of character nor do they have sound business understanding, so they should be extremely careful in matters of business and investment. But with wise self-discipline, these failings can be overcome – if only they would embrace as much discipline in their lives as they seek to impart to others. This will assist them to develop their intuition, and lead to improved happiness in their lives and in the lives of their loved ones. Generally, Ruling 7 people are rather slow learners, due to their need to experience so much for themselves. Parents should take special note of this characteristic and allow for their Ruling 7 children to learn at their own natural pace. All too often, parents regard their children's progress at school as some sort of prestige race, acting as though they were more concerned with the family name than with their child's welfare. Experience confirms that Ruling 7 children learn rapidly until around age seven, at which time they seem to need to stabilise. For the following seven years, their learning rate is noticeably slower, but from age fourteen, their academic rate will increase with appropriate self-discipline. Rarely do Ruling 7 children emerge as brilliant scholars.

○ Most suitable vocations

Trustworthy and consequently expecting trust from others, these people are well suited to positions among the judiciary and in legal practice. They are practical people with a natural flair for the use of sharp instruments, inducing many to choose careers such as surgeons, butchers and carpenters. Ruling 7s are often found as teachers and in humanitarian positions in the community, such as clergy, scientists, naturalists and philosophers.

○ Summary

Ruling 7s need to learn through personal experience, but dislike external discipline. They are assertive, philosophical and humanitarian. Their lives incur an unusually high level of sacrifice.

○ Famous Ruling 7,s

Marilyn Monroe born June 1, 1926
Peter Tchaikovsky born May 7, 1840
Cole Porter born June 9, 1891
Conrad Hilton born December 25, 1887
Germaine Greer born January 29, 1939

○ RULING NUMBER 8

These are people who regard independence as one of the most important aspects of life. They can be very complex people who invariably possess great wisdom and strength or character. Their power derives from the position of the 8 as the number of wisdom on the soul plane, as well as being in the centre of the Arrow of Activity. Ruling number 8 birth dates are those that total 17, 26, 35 or 44.

○ Life's purpose

One of the most important aspects of love is our ability to express it. One of the most vital components to successful human relationships is a fluent expression of appreciation (itself a vital embodiment of love). It is in these two avenues of expression that Ruling

8 people find greatest difficulty. Consequently, an essential feature of their purpose in life is to transcend these limitations. Growth in this direction will develop with the realisation that, rather than inhibiting their independence, such improved relationships strengthen the confidence others have in them. In turn, this creates greater personal security and improved happiness in their lives, together with growth in wisdom, which is so essential to a Ruling 8.

○ *Best expression*
Seemingly inconsistent for Ruling 8s is their enormous capacity for compassion and sympathetic tenderness for those in trouble. However, not always do they express themselves in this manner for long, tending to grow impatient with those who become dependent upon them. This, they feel, hampers their own independence. They have the ability to be enormously successful in business, particularly if they do not let their emotional misunderstandings interfere with their commercial decision making. Ruling 8 people are noticeably conscious of their dress, taking great pride in appearance, both of themselves and their loved ones. They are feeling people who often tend to hide their sensitivities until they become mature enough to express them.

○ *Distinctive traits*
A strong air of independence and dependability, together with a self-confident manner, are distinctive of Ruling 8 people. These qualities work in harmony to equip them for positions of seniority and responsibility in which many are found to excel. But their fierce independence can often transmute to an undemonstrative attitude of coolness, bordering on indifference, in the home. This is related to their difficulty in self-expression, an inhibition that

usually diminishes with maturity. Their inherent love for the more helpless creatures – animals, infants, the elderly and the sick – is constantly seeking expression and will instantly convert aloofness into loving kindness. Ruling 8s also possess a wealth of natural wisdom from which they learn to reliably draw from as they mature.

○ Negative tendencies to be surmounted

Their fierce independence is so zealously guarded that these people develop a deep resentment toward any form of (what they regard as) interference to their plans. Therefore, great diplomacy and tact should be used by those who seek to guide them. Indeed, Ruling 8 people need a great deal of guidance, especially in their handling of children – they are either overindulgent or exceptionally strict. They often find difficulty in their love relationships, tending to create a barrier and hold their feelings in close check. As they mature, they realise how much happier they can be with the natural expression of their loving feelings.

○ Recommended development

Every effort should be made to overcome the undemonstrativeness they so often exhibit towards their loved ones. This is best achieved through awareness of its existence, for many Ruling 8 people do not see themselves as undemonstrative. As they learn to express their feelings more fluently, their happiness and personal security improve. Appreciation, expressed in the first person, is an excellent means of developing the expression of their deeper feelings. With this growth will develop the overall wisdom that, hitherto, they have tended only to express in impersonal situations, such as in business or in giving advice to others. Their wisdom and maturity will be enhanced through travel, of which they are very fond.

○ *Most suitable vocations*

Ruling 8s are often found at the head of large business undertakings, or as senior executives with excellent prospects. They have a sound understanding of finance and are attracted to banking, stockbroking, and so on. They will also be found as travel executives, aircraft and ship's captains, teachers and nurses to children or the elderly, working with animals or as senior figures of humane organisations. Due to their tendency to mask their natural feelings, many become successful at professional acting (which comes natural to them as they tend to be acting throughout their entire lives).

○ **Summary**

They are independent, highly dependable, self-confident, undemonstrative, commercially oriented and deeply concerned for the sick and the helpless.

○ *Famous Ruling 8's*

Joan Collins born May 23, 1933

Elizabeth Taylor born February 27, 1932

Boris Yeltsin born February 1, 1931

Nelson Mandela born July 18, 1918

Paul Newman born January 5, 1946

Liza Minnelli born March 12, 1946

Jane Fonda born December 21, 1937

○ **RULING NUMBER 9**

The humanitarian qualities of ambition, responsibility and idealism are the three-fold aspects of Ruling 9 people, whose prime motivation is to put people before things. They are individuals whose birth date numbers total 18, 27, 36 or 45.

○ *Life's purpose*

This is a powerful mind number implying a constant responsibility among those who have it. They are far more suited to art than to science, to humanitarian rather than to commercial pursuits. Many of our cultural leaders and serious actors are found with this Ruling Number, all of whom are idealists at heart, though their concepts are not always the most workable. It is an important aspect of their purpose in life to learn to translate the idealistic into the practical.

○ *Best expression*

To serve humanity and improve human life are at the very heart of a Ruling 9's expression. The method by which they can best achieve this will be found from the analysis of their Birth Chart (see chapter 5) and Pyramids (see Chapter11). These people are ambitious, but are inclined to be more concerned with the overall plan than its details. They are thus more suited to non-commercial undertakings, as they tend to be poor financial managers, especially in their personal affairs. They are very artistic, preferring the deeply serious to the comic or popular forms of artistic expression.

○ *Distinctive traits*

Ambition, responsibility and idealism are their progressive growth qualities, but through it all, the heavy emphasis is on personal responsibility. Honesty is so natural to them that they assume everyone to be so inclined. This often leads to significant disappointments in people, and some Ruling 9s have been known to develop a deep cynicism as a consequence, even to the extent of doubting the wisdom of their own honesty. They find it easier to give money to the needy, rather than save it for themselves, and this often gives rise to expressions of frustration from their partners. They have very definite thoughts about life and its ideals, about humanity and how people should be motivated. Though these ideas are not always the most practical, Ruling 9s will strive to implement them, such is the nature of their ambitiousness and idealism.

○ Negative tendencies to be surmounted

An indication of negative living is when these people fail to adopt the ideals they seek to impress on others. They need to take great care to ensure they do not fall victim to one of the most offensive of all human traits, that of hypocrisy. Their ambitions can dominate and destroy the integrity of their ideals, thereby developing an egocentricity that is far from appealing. This will often produce a very abrupt manner and an attitude of destructive criticism, which the people in their lives will find difficult to tolerate, and which can ultimately lead to their undoing when they are materially motivated.

○ Recommended development

The strong idealism of the Ruling 9 does not make for successful judges of character. Yet once this limitation is realised, it can be remedied by the study and employment of a reliable guide such as numerology that can help them to understand people. This will assist them to investigate all aspects of a person before drawing conclusions based solely on their personal analysis. In turn, this study will help Ruling 9 people develop their intuition and wisdom. Patience and persistence are two other important traits these people need to develop. As they appear to the world, Ruling 9s are seen as overly serious – they need to laugh more and enjoy humour as a vital balance to life.

○ Most suitable vocations

Ruling 9s will be found happily working in religious disciplines, welfare organisations, educational institutions (as administrators rather than teachers), research facilities (including computers), crime solving, the healing professions and as counsellors. Many will be found in professional acting and artistic careers, but in the more serious aspects of them. They rarely excel as senior business executives.

○ Summary

Ruling 9s are eminently responsible, extremely honest, idealistic, ambitious, humanitarian and very serious about life. They have difficulty saving money.

○ Famous Ruling 9's

Shirley Maclaine born April 24, 1934
Joan Sutherland born November 7, 1926
Elvis Presley born January 8, 1935
Linda Evans born November 18, 1942
Burt Lancaster born November 2, 1913
Jimmy Carter born October 1, 1924
Richard Harris born October 1, 1933

○ RULING NUMBER 10

Most Ruling numbers can be expressed in a variety of ways, depending on the degree of awareness of the person. But there is no greater range of expression than that found in the potential of the Ruling 10. They vary from the most likeable, personality-plus people when living positively, to lost, floundering, insecure beings when negativity takes over. They are the most adaptable people. They have the potential for brilliant success or they can languish in mediocrity. Birth dates with totals of 19, 28, 37 or 46 are Ruling 10s.

○ Life's purpose

Adaptability and adjustment are the keynotes of the Ruling 10's life. Their innate flexibility can be of enormous assistance when it comes to helping others adjust to life's many changes. As life becomes more complex, human adaptation becomes more vital, and so we find Ruling 10 people in a wide diversity of vocations and situations. They have a natural fearlessness that often leads them into pioneering ventures others would never consider undertaking.

○ Best expression

If we want someone to assist us to enjoy the light-hearted pleasures of life, we need look no further than a Ruling 10 person. They express best when allowed the freedom to experience what they regard as the bubbling excitement of life. But when they are suppressed or feel emotionally hampered, they become despondent without realising why. This gives rise to frustration, often evidenced by irritability or a short temper. The minority of Ruling 10 people will be constantly forthright, non-reactive and clearly assertive – their optimism knows no bounds, leading them to achieve remarkable progress in life. This is the natural expression of the Ruling 10, being the powerful combination of the ego (the 1), expressing its infinite spiritual depth through the 0.

○ Distinctive traits

Essentially a physical (doing) Ruling Number, the 10 endows a power of flexibility and adaptability that produces a highly popular personality. Their generally happy disposition is quite contagious, yet because they prefer to avoid delving deeply into other people's problems, they find it difficult to understand why others are not as happy and well-adjusted as they like to be. The majority of Ruling 10s rarely delves deeply into life, more content with more superficial pleasures, particularly sports – either actively or passively. By contrast, the aware minority of Ruling 10s will become successful and dominant in their profession, for they have a depth of fortitude that enables them to rise above some of the most difficult conditions. In general, Ruling 10 people unconsciously adopt an air of debonair self-assurance, reflected in their personal confidence and their elegant appearance, no matter how they dress. They are not so successful in solving mental problems in their life or the lives of others, and do not make good counsellors or deep, meaningful friendships, often preferring the company of members of their own sex to that of the opposite sex. They are generally artistic, with a very sensitive touch that make, them competent instrumentalists and capable judges of quality in clothing and materials.

○ *Negative tendencies to be surmounted*

Their self-confidence can sometimes lead these people to dominate others, but they do so unwisely, invariably creating a disharmony more intense than they sought to overcome. This tendency is best avoided through better control of the ego, recognising the depth of spiritual substance and avoiding superficiality in their lives. Engagement in constructive and creative activities will significantly assist Ruling 10 people to adopt a more penetrative perspective on life, and the recognition that if doors close in their face, they need to turn around and find other open doors. They must avoid being lazy and expecting life to be one big ball; and they must recognise the need to develop self-discipline to overcome melancholy and emotional insecurity.

○ *Recommended development*

Ruling 10 people have the tendency to become lost in conformity and to be accepting of mediocrity as the norm. They need to recognise their potential for the exceptional, their versatility and their profound adaptability. Throughout their lives, they need to practise meditation to centre themselves and bring them in touch with their inner strength. They should also employ temperance (balance) in their lives, and develop awareness of the world surrounding them (erudition), harmony in their attitudes, compassion and reverence for life. Also, developing discrimination between important and unimportant prospects in their life is important, otherwise they can waste considerable time in worthless pursuits.

○ *Most suitable vocations*

The fields of professional sports or entertainment, interior decorating and design, and work with fabrics or food are good vocations for Ruling 10s. Also, they make good salespeople (where they are invariably irresistible), politicians, charity fundraisers, business executives, sales managers, town planners, architects and real estate agents.

○ *Summary*

They are confident, debonair, bright and happy people, with an extremely sensitive touch and an amazing ability to sell.

○ *Famous Ruling 10's*

Rupert Murdoch born March 11, 1931
Jack Nicholson born April 22, 1937
Sophia Loren born September 20, 1943
Henry Ford born July 30, 1863
Jerry Lewis born March 16, 1926
Billy Joel born May 9, 1949

○ RULING NUMBER 11

An especially high level of spirituality surrounds this Ruling Number, offering those born to it a unique potential for developing the awareness of the high self. Unfortunately, more people fail to live up to this potential power than develop it, but this pattern is changing with the rapid approach of the new age of enlightenment (New Age). Though we do not find many Ruling 11s as most of the other numbers, they certainly proliferate in domains where personal growth and spiritual upliftment predominate (and they will all be reading this book!). In practice, only two birth date totals commonly qualify for Ruling number 11 – that is 29 and 38 – though an occasional birth date total of 47 will be found.

○ Life's purpose

These people are among the few who are potentially best equipped to guide humanity into the emerging age of awareness. It is a very responsible incarnation they have chosen. Unfortunately, many find that they are enticed (through their basic self) by life's physical attractions and are thus diverted from their higher purpose. But the tide is changing as the real values of life gain credence over manipulation and the false prophets.

○ Best expression

As lovers of refinement, beauty and the cultural values of life, Ruling 11 people naturally gravitate toward such an environment because it liberates them to express their innate beauty and spirituality. Material life, for them, can be demanding and uninteresting (unless they choose to live under their Day Number – see chapter 8 – or give in to peer-group pressure). But they have to learn to balance the material with the ideals they seek within to realise that the noblest of spiritual virtues is of little value unless it can be employed to improve the quality of life. No finer expression can be found than in doing this.

○ *Distinctive traits*

There are extreme differences between the lifestyles of the Ruling 11s who live positively and utilise their exceptional spiritual powers and the negative counterpart whose life appears difficult and colourless. An uncompromisingly high level of morality and ethics, a profoundly reliable intuitiveness, and an inspired driving force are clearly in evidence when these people are involved in spiritually-oriented pursuits. When they are living naturally they are deeply feeling people, extremely dependable, honest and just, with a deep love for family and friends and a sincere compassion for all life.

○ *Negative tendencies to be surmounted*

The temptation to abdicate our responsibility for virtuous living becomes stronger as modern commercialism seeks new and more devious avenues to flog its overproduction of often unnecessary commodities. Life is meant to be far less complicated, far more harmonious than many people currently realise. Such complexities can easily confuse and misdirect people from their path. When this occurs, they tend to become bitter and spiteful, often indifferent in their attitude toward other people and their work. When it occurs in the life of a Ruling 11, they become lost and apathetic, finding little solace in the material world into which they have become enticed. They must employ great awareness and care to be firm in their resolves to keep to their path, for it will not be difficult so long as they take unbiased note of their profound intuition.

○ *Recommended development*

Spiritual faculties do not easily mix with commerce for the Ruling 11. Consequently, their best avenues for expression lie in those professions that facilitate growth in spiritual awareness and give substance to their noble sensitivities. At the same time, adequate monetary rewards are essential, so a compromise is often in order. With their natural generosity and sensitivity to the needs of others, Ruling 11s often find an above-average demand on their financial resources. They have to learn not only the most practical means of expressing their spirituality, but also to be guided by intuition rather than motivated by base desires (such as for recognition, reward or return favours). The practice of such disciplines as discrimination, temperance and fortitude will significantly assist them. They are often tempted to reject assistance for themselves when in need, but must learn to be more receptive and to recognise the benefits that can accrue from such practical cooperation.

○ *Most suitable vocations*

Educators, social workers, religious leaders and personal growth instructors are often found to be Ruling 11s. Others capably turn to the teaching of cultural subjects, exploration and the field of professional performing, so long as their roles have underlying moral values. Their intuition can also qualify them to become amazing designers or inventors.

○ *Summary*

Sensitive, feeling and caring people are the Ruling 11s. They love refinement, beauty and everything with a depth of cultural substance; and are intensely honest and compassionate, often preferring to avoid the life of hard business for they are generally not competent money managers.

○ *Famous Ruling 11's*

Wolfgang Amadeus mozart born january 27, 1756
Prince Charles born november 14, 1948
Anthony Newley born september 24, 1931

Jacqueline Kennedy onassis born July 28, 1929

Tony Bennett born August 3, 1926

Sir Edmund Hillary born July 20, 1919

John Glenn born July 18, 1921

Eartha Kitt born January 26, 1928

○ RULING NUMBER 22/4

This is the master number. People born as 22/4s have almost limitless potential and often make their mark in life by achieving seemingly impossible goals. But there are two distinctly different Ruling 22/4s – the aware and the unaware. The difference between them is as extreme as the power of the number. The former benefit from the successful mastery of any aspect of life into which they are directed; the latter drift into a lazy indifference, becoming almost useless misfits, many of them drifting into mental institutions. Only one total of birth date numbers resolves to a Ruling number 22/4 and that is the total of 22, occurring only with some one to two percent of the population.

○ *Life's purpose*

As human life continues to evolve through progressive stages of enlightenment, there will always be people of outstanding leadership whose purpose is to guide such evolution. This they achieve in much the same way as some outstanding directors guide the unfolding of a movie or a play. They might take a minor role in it themselves, but rarely the starring role, preferring to guide from behind the scenes, where the decisions are made and the entire overall design is formulated. In whatever area of life they find themselves, Ruling 22/4s are invariably at the centre when living positively. In this new age of awareness, the role of these people becomes crucial, for their personal enlightenment is a beacon whose life will illumine the Path and guide countless others, many of whom will be unaware of the source. For centuries, 22/4s consistently chose to work behind the scenes, but as life evolves, more and more 22/4s are coming to the fore to take charge of events as the course becomes treacherous. They ask only for respect and cooperation to facilitate their work.

○ *Best expression*

To achieve any semblance of their potential, Ruling 22/4 people need a first-rate education. Many spend a great deal of time at their studies, continually seeking to better themselves and to satisfy their inner craving for knowledge. They realise that by this means they are better equipped to guide others. Ruling 22/4s must be able to work without constrictions to achieve their best, for they become most frustrated if working under dominant direction for too long. The rate at which they learn is little short of amazing, as though they have accomplished most things in past lives and are merely re-acquainting themselves with the current modes of expression. Little wonder they rise to leadership so often in life and are constantly called on for advice and guidance.

○ *Distinctive traits*

One of the most noticeable traits of the Ruling 22/4 is their apparent lack of emotion. They regard emotional control as fundamental to their purpose, and adopt it to minimise reactive behaviour rather than to appear detached or difficult to understand. Actually, they are very sensitive, highly intuitive people who combine the unique abilities of powerful spiritual awareness (the double 11) with the eminently practical 4. They rarely fail to accept a challenge, especially if it involves human welfare. They will be found in some of the most difficult and seemingly dangerous environments, but are usually cool and careful in the execution of whatever work they are directing. Their capacity for responsibility is almost limitless, consequently some people habitually depend on them, often thoughtlessly.

○ Negative tendencies to be surmounted

Most Ruling 22/4s readily recognise many of their strengths and capably employ them. The few who do not or who are drawn into a singularly materialistic environment, take on all the negative aspects of the Ruling 4, but worse. In so doing, they become little better than misfits, with an obsession for money, in the quest for which they will brook little interference, becoming unhappy, aloof and lonely. Rehabilitation from these depths demands great patience, understanding and loving tenderness, for the 22/4 can become the most depressed person when negative (the opposite end of the scale to the dynamic achiever). As all Ruling 22/4s are fond of art, rhythm, dancing and most forms of music, the wise use of these forms of expression will greatly help to bring about balanced emotions and a more positive attitude. This will bring them out of their self-centred world and help them to regain their positive outlook on life.

○ Recommended development

For all Ruling 22/4 people, it is vital to ensure that life provides a balance of work and pleasure. Their considerable aptitude for work often causes them to become obsessed with achieving, to the detriment of quality family, hobby and relaxation time. Their development along artistic lines through hobbies – such as singing, dancing, painting, writing and so on – will enhance the expression of their feelings and relax them emotionally. They must realise they are never too old to learn, for learning is a lifelong pursuit for them.

○ *Most suitable vocations*

These people are suited to work as leaders in practically any business or cultural organisation. They excel at whatever they attempt, be it in art, writing, politics, the diplomatic services... or as efficiency experts, humanitarians, technicians (especially with computers) or teachers.

○ *Summary*

This is the master number whose bearers have the most responsibility to humanity. They are self-confident, highly intuitive and sensitive, with a tight rein on their emotions and an intense concern for human welfare. They have to take care not to become ruthless in their pursuit of their goals.

○ *Famous Ruling 22/4's*

Margaret Thatcher born October 13, 1925

Richard Wagner born May 22, 1813

Frank Sinatra born December 12, 1915

Luciano Pavarotti born October 12, 1935

Clint Eastwood born May 31, 1930

CHAPTER .08

The Day Numbers

We often witness attempts in nature and society to achieve balance. Winds are created to balance atmospheric air pressures; night and day permit us to balance our energy levels (activity during the day, rest at night); and in the financial arena, economic inflation has to give way to recession.

Human personality seeks balance in the grand scheme of things. We know that our primary pathway in life is revealed by our Ruling Number, but we must also realise that we are not intended to singularly or fanatically pursue this pathway without both a measure of relief and diversion that permits the development of a lesser aspect of our individuality. Such is the purpose of our Day Number – the number of the actual day of the month on which we were born.

Just as it is important for us to develop the understanding of our eternal being, the inner self, so is it necessary for us to understand the manner by which we express to the world through the outer self. We do this through our Day Number and our name (see Chapter 12).

With most birth dates, the Day Number is different to the Ruling Number. Yet for some people it is the same number. In these instances, the apparent need to strengthen your Ruling Number clearly outweighs the need to divert from it, circumstances derived from the previous one or two lifetimes. (If you find this explanation incredible, do not dismiss it until you have had the opportunity to investigate it for yourself. Most Westerners have not recognised the significance of karmically-created traits in their current personality.)

To prepare it for proper analysis, each Day Number is treated in the same basic manner as is the Ruling Number. Each double number of a day on which a person is born is resolved to a single number by simple addition, with the same exceptions as the Ruling Number. However, there is one additional exception for a Day Number and it occurs when a person is born on the first day of the month. We do not have a Ruling Number 1, but we certainly have a Day Number 1. To avoid any misunderstandings, all Day Numbers are listed:

Day born	Day Number
○ 1st day of month	1
○ 2nd day of month	2
○ 3rd day of month	3
○ 4th day of month	4
○ 5th day of month	5
○ 6th day of month	6
○ 7th day of month	7
○ 8th day of month	8
○ 9th day of month	9
○ 10th day of month	10
○ 11th day of month	11
○ 12th day of month	3
○ 13th day of month	4
○ 14th day of month	5

○ 15th day of month 6

○ 16th day of month 7

○ 17th day of month 8

○ 18th day of month 9

○ 19th day of month 10

○ 20th day of month 2

○ 21st day of month 3

○ 22nd day of month 22/4

○ 23rd day of month 5

○ 24th day of month 6

○ 25th day of month 7

○ 26th day of month 8

○ 27th day of month 9

○ 28th day of month 10

○ 29th day of month 11

○ 30th day of month 3

○ 31st day of month 4

Because each number has the same basic properties, a Day Number will have similar aspects to its identical Ruling Number, except that the Ruling Number is naturally the stronger. It is important to realise that the Day Number is intended to represent our alternate other self. Thus, when people choose to align themselves more with its power than that of their Ruling Number, their lives will ultimately fall apart.

○ DAY NUMBER 1

People born on the first day of the month always do their best when allowed to work on their own. They need ample freedom to fully develop and express their unique initiative. The direction in which to channel this expression is indicated by their Ruling Number though they are sometimes tempted to depart from its direction as they want to do things their way. Because of their preference for individual effort, these people can appear aloof or detached for certain periods. This is especially noticeable in children born on the first day of the month – it should cause no alarm, for it is merely their other self enjoying its seclusion.

○ DAY NUMBER 2

This brings with it added intuitiveness, which is a valuable benefit in decision-making. It also stimulates the desire to work closely with someone who has a bright, happy disposition. These people enjoy light entertainment, especially if humorous, preferring to be entertained than do the entertaining. They are reliable, supportive people who are generally happy and light hearted, preferring the natural to the artificial.

○ DAY NUMBER 3

Opposite to the previous Day Number, these people are the fun-loving entertainers. Most of them only want to be involved in projects on a part-time basis, for they often have other more vital things to pursue in line with their life purpose (as indicated by their Ruling Number). They are people who thoroughly enjoy all forms of humour, especially satirical humour. They are generally bright extroverts with a very active brain and a ready answer, but they do have an underlying tendency to be critical of more sombre people without attempting to understand the nature of these different personalities. Care should be taken to resist the destructive urge to criticise. Instead, subtle humour can be used to get a point across if they believe the other person needs help. Sometimes it is they who need the help.

○ Day number 4

A practical and capable flair helps these people to express themselves well with their hands or feet. If their Ruling Number is an odd number, this Day Number will assist them to create balance, with the adoption of a predominantly artistic or philosophical approach to life. Should their Ruling Number be an even number, they need to take care to avoid any undue emphasis on materialism, and learn that they will achieve the best results from their actions when they employ the patient ability to organise, which is second nature to the Day Number 4.

○ Day number 5

These are caring, compassionate people for whom it is essential to have the freedom to express their deep feelings. They are sensitive and yet possess a balance that underlies their ability to achieve success and happiness, provided they do not develop a fear of being misunderstood. This could produce a shyness that inhibits their true self-expression, causing an inward intensity due to suppressed natural expressions. They need to engage in plenty of outdoor exercise and activity, and to select bright company with whom they can freely share laughter and the joy of living.

○ Day number 6

Though this is a number of creativity, for most people such expression seems to be restricted to the domestic sphere. This is especially so in the case of women, though men also tend to prefer to stay at home, doing little things of a creative nature rather than be out with their mates. Its positive expression is of love and beauty, qualities that make the Day Number 6 a person to brighten up the home or the work place. When living negatively, these people take on the worry syndrome, over-dramatising domestic problems and developing all sorts of fears and anxieties with a dreary, almost never ending habit of complaining. Their panacea is readily found by replacing the worry habit with creativity. For example, by engaging in some form of productive hobby such as painting, pottery, music, and so on.

○ DAY NUMBER 7

No number provides a more active understanding of life's lessons than the 7. Its special purpose is to induce personal involvement which the person learns the lessons of life in the most indelible way – through personal sacrifice. This will usually affect the pocket more than health or love, though the latter two will be involved if the lessons are not readily recognised. As these people mature in wisdom, they will feel drawn to share their life's experiences in a practical way through teaching. In this way, the profound lessons of this number can be successfully instilled upon the soul.

○ DAY NUMBER 8

Humans tend to work and act as part of a group, so accustomed are they to being organised and directed. But this ultimately becomes the antithesis to the development of personal independence, the primary purpose of this Day Number. As these people grow in personal awareness, they will recognise an emerging need for the independent expression of their feelings, emotions and intuition. This essential independence is the basis upon which all other forms of personal expression will. However, some people will tend to misconstrue financial independence as the basis and to go resolutely for this, rather than recognise it as a development of the successful acquisition of independence of the self. Unless financial success is based on a mature understanding of their personal life, such prosperity will be somewhat temporary.

○ Day number 9

In its more limited role as a Day Number, the 9 expresses itself primarily as the symbol of responsibility, motivated by idealism. As such, it assists us to realise the purpose of our experiences with other people. This tends to imply a rather serious role in our affairs, but it is not intended that we be constantly serious, as are so many people with this Day Number. If such is the case, they should seek bright and happy company, learning to have fun and laugh more to maintain that vital emotional balance. Some people tend to become overly ambitious under the influence of the Day 9, but if this is not directed toward the common good, it can produce its own form of instability through dissatisfaction. People with this Day Number should be careful to avoid intense arguments, for their over serious-ness tends to induce a fanaticism that borders on mental instability as they lose control of reason. Better they learn to express any personal differences within the context of a discussion.

○ Day number 10

That power of happy adaptability at the foundation of easygoing friendship is profuse with these people. They are gregarious, ener-getic, generous and easily pleased, usually with an abundant num-ber of acquaintances whose similar desires provide constant phys-ical gratification. But they need to guard against a tendency to superficiality, for this inhibits the development of worthwhile friendships and restricts their personal understanding of the real purpose of life. Extravagance with their time, energy and or money might make them the centre of attention for a time, but such protracted wastefulness will inevitably result in emptiness. They should be prepared to use their talents to develop their primary purpose in life, as revealed by their Ruling Number.

○ DAY NUMBER 11

The high level of spirituality with which this number is identified usually finds its best expression through intuition as a Day Number. This is potentially a thoroughly reliable guide to the understanding of people and events, but only when free of high emotion. Unfortunately, a tendency of so many Day Number 11 people is to become involved in emotional extremes, such as are expressed in moodiness, anxiety or abruptness. These emotions are extremely enervating and unhealthy. They should be controlled as soon as they are recognised, for they can be easily transformed to become positive spiritual guidance. This allows the Day Number 11's intuition to develop to its ultimate glory as thorough reliability.

○ DAY NUMBER 22/4

The potential power of this number is second to none, for it combines intuition with the practical, leading to the ready recognition that the achievement of anything is possible. But this will only become a reality if the person has achieved a comprehensive integration over the three Planes: Mind, Soul and Physical. Otherwise, the use of this power can become lopsidedly motivated by the base desire to attain control for the sake of the power it brings. Such is the temptation for people of this Day Number. But such reliance can only lead to ultimate fragmentation, with resultant loss intended to convey the lesson that one's Day Number is essentially an alternate power and is never intended to be the primary seat of influence.

○ WORD OF CAUTION

Throughout this chapter on the Day Numbers, I have stressed the importance of recognising them as aspects of our other side, our alternate self, as this is the supportive side of our individuality. For any number of reasons, people are sometimes induced to primary motivation by the power of their Day Number rather than that of their Ruling Number, and when this persists in their lives it invites danger.

Resultant problems usually arise from an emerging instability where the individual's material life becomes fragmented as they lose money and friends. Simultaneously, they become emotionally insecure and mentally unstable. Many such people are in dire need of appropriate counselling, some gravitating to institutions specialising in full-time care. Yet rarely do private counsellors or practitioners in such institutions realise the personality "flip" that has occurred as a result of the individual's inappropriate focus on how they express their individuality based on the temporary power of their Day Number.

Treatment would be so much more effective, inexpensive and quicker if such professionals were also practitioners of numerology, for it is far more scientific and reliable than many of the arts they currently use, such as psychological assessments. To understand how the patient has departed from the primary power of the Ruling Number is to be well on the way to effecting a lasting recovery. This is usually best achieved by teaching the patient to re-develop (because they often identified with the qualities of their Ruling Number earlier in life) the essential aspects indicated by their Ruling Number, and in turn teaching them the most appropriate ways to express themselves, physically, mentally and emotionally.

CHAPTER .09

The 9-year cycle of change

"THERE IS A TIDE IN THE AFFAIRS OF MEN,
WHICH, TAKEN AT THE FLOOD, LEADS ON TO FORTUNE."
– William Shakespeare (Julius Caesar, IV, iii)

Life was not meant to be boring. Indeed, for those already on the Path, it is anything but. Those approaching their Path, or vacillating on and off it, find plenty of variety adds spice to their lives, albeit some of which proves most frustrating until they get their lives in orders. Few people these days are boring enough to languish in a rut of monotony, unlike the lives of many in bygone centuries when variety and opportunity were far less prevalent.

Consequently, it has come to pass that in this modern age, a lot more people are able to take advantage of the diverse aspects of their personality and express themselves with a freedom hitherto virtually unknown in the history of this planet. Not that such diversity is new per se, but that its expression is considerably less inhibited.

From our study of numerology, we know that human personality has always had potentially diverse aspects. These are revealed by the Day Number, the numbers (or their lack) on the Birth Chart and the Personal Year Numbers, leading as they do to the Pyramids (see Chapter 10).

There are two significant aspects to the understanding of personal numerology: the basic and the flexible. The numbers of our birth date provide the basic aspects, while the flexible aspects are the cyclic variations that fall within the ambit of the Personal Year Cycles and, within them, the monthly cycles.

We have all found that some years of our lives exemplify progress while others become remembered for their time-consuming annoyances. Our memory seems to cling to these extremes. However, were the memory more reliable and more cognizant of other than extremes, we would also recall those years of stabilising quietude when no significant material progress or frustration occurred. We would also have detected cycles of change running through our lives.

These Cycles facilitate the progress we are able to achieve as we evolve through that endless lesson book entitled *Life on Earth*. Recognising as we do that the purpose of human life is to evolve toward perfection, it is fundamental to our understanding that such evolvement imply growth. And growth demands change.

Every form on Earth, be it animate or inanimate, experiences constant change. Rocks, oceans, mountains and deserts are all undergoing change, albeit over extremely long time cycles. Plants, birds, animals, humans and all other living forms are constantly undergoing stages of far more rapid change.

Uniquely, of all life forms, humans alone are endowed with the inherent ability to exercise some form of control over their change, both in substance and time. But how we handle this distinctive ability is very much an individual expression and, all too often, one that is largely ignored.

Unfortunately, many people tend to react to change or attempt to totally resist it, thereby inducing physical pain, which is clearly our resistance to change. We all need to become courageous to venture beyond our comfort zone by taking affirmative action to attain optimum benefits from inevitable change.

Change is more than accepting minor variations in your lifestyle. It necessitates that we embrace personal courage, the very antithesis of frustration and boredom. So what do we have to lose?

Why is it that millions of people throughout the world continue to fear change? All they do is make a token motion toward the improvement of their lot in life, generally ignoring the major opportunities that come their way time and again.

The excitement of change that is felt by most people during their later years of adolescence and their earlier years of maturity (20s and 30s) often diminishes to complacency as they reach their 40s and 50sWhile in their 60's, they often not only retire from work, but also life. During these progressive years of maturity, when great strides can be taken to develop personal financial success with the underpinning of past experience and accumulated wisdom, so many people lapse into mental slumber. As their excitement for life wanes, so does the life force in their bodies. It is then that they commence their descent toward death, a protracted journey that might last a decade or two but one that did not have to be (see Chapter 10).

The recognition of our Personal Year Cycles and guiding our lives successfully through them distinguishes the exceptional from the average person. We have all known exceptional people in whose presence we feel uplifted; at times their success may cause us to experience a touch of envy. They might not have had the advantage of understanding about their Personal Year Numbers, but they certainly had the intuition and the wisdom to go with the flow in their lives.

Indeed, we all like to win in life, but too few are prepared to be winners. Is it because we are so uncertain of the foundation of our success? Now, with this insight into individual Personal Year Numbers, we can reliably chart our course with a dependable expectation of its outcome. Here, at our disposal, is a proven technique to aid the transition from average human to exceptional, such that the exceptional becomes the norm.

Once we arrive at the point in our lives where we recognise and understand these cycles of change, we find it to our advantage to cooperate with them. This is not to imply that we become enslaved to them, any more than the apple tree is enslaved to the seasons as they are calculated on the calendar. But when we recognise the necessity of change, we take advantage of its offering, just as the apple tree might blossom early in spring if the weather is unusually warm.

These changes are necessary to allow us suitable periods for growth on each of our three vital levels – physical, spiritual and mental. Such growth must always be followed by periods of stabilisation, and consolidation during which the preceding period of development can be properly assimilated.

Personal Year Cycles are not haphazard occurrences. They are very carefully planned by the same creative force that governs everything that is created. With the recognition of these cycles, we become more aware of the divine plan of life, learning not to expect each year to be one of dynamic progress and material gain. If we recognise each year for its particular aspect of growth or stability, we are equipped to wisely select our activities in accordance with our need for physical, spiritual or mental development. More progress is always achieved by swimming with the current than by fighting against it.

Cycles of change penetrate every aspect of life. The twenty four hour daynight cycle is designed to alternate growth and rest over a comparatively short period. The four-season year facilitates growth and rest over a larger time span. Both cycles are governed by the sun and that too has cycles of change.

Planet Earth has annual cycles too. Its years of change synchronise with the nine-year cycle that applies to human evolution. Every nine years, a complete cycle is made, with changes occurring each year within the cycle as one month inexorably glides into the next. For human life and our planet, the nature of the influence of each year is symbolised by successive year numbers. For humans, these are called "Personal Year Numbers"; for the planet they are known as "World Year Numbers."

To fully understand this progression, we must accept our present calendar system. From it, we can interpret other systems if we so desire. But let us first perfect the one we know and use, realising that all calendar systems are in harmony with each other and with those they have succeeded.

With our current global system of time measurement, we find that the nine-year cycle numbers continue relentlessly through this Christian era in exactly the same manner as they did in the preceding Roman, Greek and Hebrew calendars. There is a slight variation in the meaning of the numbers, as would be expected when we recognise the modifications in lifestyles, attitudes and consciousness brought about by the birth of Christianity and, subsequently, of personal awareness in the new millennium.

Analysing World Year Numbers gives an interesting guide to general trends, but only when these are applied to the world's decision makers do we attain the full picture of what to expect and how to understand what has occurred. Before we can obtain individual Personal Year Numbers, we must calculate World Year Numbers for the year in question. Let's take the following examples:

$$2003 = 2 + 0 + 0 + 3 = 5$$
$$2004 = 2 + 0 + 0 + 4 = 6$$
$$2005 = 2 + 0 + 0 + 5 = 7$$
$$2006 = 2 + 0 + 0 + 6 = 8$$

Thus, the World Year Numbers for the above four years are 5, 6, 7 and 8 respectively. The cycle of World Year Numbers runs from 1 to 9 consecutively, then back to 1 for the following cycle through to 9 again, and so on. During certain decades, the World Year Number of 4 became a 22/4 vibration, as in the years 1894, 1939, 1948, 1957, 1966, 1975, 1984 and 1993 – it won't happen again until the year 2299.

The power exerted by the 22/4 vibration will always leave its mark on world history, especially when it includes the powerful idealism (or ambition) of the double-9, as in the years 1939 and 1993. The unbridled ambition of a German dictator in the 1930s caused an ill-prepared Britain to declare war on him when the third 9 combined with the imagination of the double 3 – on September 3, 1939. We experienced the same set of vibrations in the 1990s with the emergence of another dictator who, from most reports, is no less ruthless in venting his ambition upon the world. Saddam Hussein has tried twice (in Iran and Kuwait) to conquer, but his personal numbers were even more powerful in 1993, – a 22/4 World Year Number when his Personal Year Number was an ambitious 9 and he was at a significant peak on his Pyramids (see Chapter 10).

The World Year Number prevails for the duration of the calendar year (January 1 through December 31). This clearly indicates that our Personal Year Numbers are functions of the calendar year, irrespective of how far into the year our birth date might fall. Thus, whether a person's birth date falls on January 12 or December 1, they still share the identical Personal Year Number each year. Approximately 11 percent of the world's population has the same Personal Year Number each year, so never feel alone.

As an example of how easy it is to calculate anyone's Personal Year Numbers, let us use the birth date of 12/27/1998. A person with such a birth date has a Ruling Number 3 and in 1998a

Personal Year Number of 3. But in 1999, this person's Personal Year Number was 4, while her Ruling Number remained unchanged as 3, and will continue to be so for the of her life. Her successive Personal Year Numbers for the four years of World Year Numbers (WYN) we used in the previous example are:

○ 2002 = WYN 4 + MONTH (12) + DAY (27) =
4 + 1 + 2 + 2 + 7 = 16; 1 + 6 = 7

○ 2003 = WYN 5 + 1 + 2 + 2 + 7 = 17; 1 + 7 = 8

○ 2004 = WYN 6 + 1 + 2 + 2 + 7 = 18; 1 + 8 = 9

○ 2005 = WYN 7 + 1 + 2 + 2 + 7 = 19; 1 + 9 = 10;
1 + 0 = 1

So her Personal Year Numbers for these four years are 7, 8, 9 and 1 respectively, while the World Year Numbers appear as 4, 5, 6 and 7.

○ CHARTING THE PERSONAL YEAR CYCLE

Similar to depicting the cycle of any waveform (electrical, sound, light, and so on), the Personal Year cycle, with its peaks and troughs can be graphically represented as:

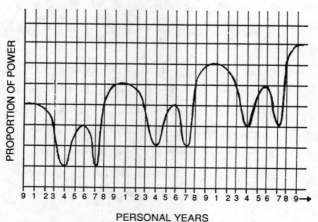

PERSONAL YEARS

It is clearly seen that the Personal Years 9 and 1 collectively form the major peak in the cycle, while the Personal Year 6 forms a minor peak. The trough years are represented by the Personal Years 4 and 7. Remember not to regard those trough years as "bad" years, but as consolidating or stabilising years that only become difficult if we attempt to move against the flow and make major changes or seek continued progress in those years.

Another vital observation is that each successive cycle progresses higher than the previous. On the graph, the second Personal Year 9 is more powerful than the previous peak of nine. Likewise, successive troughs do not plunge as far down the power scale as their predecessors. This progression is symbolic of our growth through life, though the degree of progress will vary from person to person and rarely be as uniform as the average depicted on the above graph.

Each Personal Year Number (PYN) plays a natural role in our life's unfolding. And within each year, each month asserts its own influence such that our ability to chart a more successful path in our lives is as readily at our disposal as are road maps for the motorist who is about to travel over unfamiliar territory. As a road map reveals to us which direction to take, the nature of the terrain and what we are to expect along the journey, so the understanding of our PYNs similarly prepare us for greater success throughout life's journey.

As can be readily seen from the following explanations of each of the PYNs and their monthly variations, such direction is uniquely invaluable. It is unique because this guidance is based on Pythagorean numerology (Science of Numbers), modified and updated for this era over the past 60 years, first by my master teacher, Hettie Templeton, then by me in the further development of her work. It is invaluable because it assists each of us to direct our lives more accurately toward success, rather than zigzagging from one disaster to another over most of our years. Through understanding our lives, we have solved one of the greatest of all puzzles.

○ PERSONAL YEAR 9 THE PEAK YEAR OF CHANGE

We commence by analysing this year first, because it is both the end of the old cycle and the commencement of the new. At the forefront of the major peak in the nine-year Personal Year cycle, it is the year in which change is set into motion. However, many aspects of the changes will not always be realised until later in the year or during the following year. These changes will vary considerably over the lifetime of each person, becoming especially pronounced during the twenty-seven year duration of developing maturity through the Pyramids (see Chapter 10).

General aspects of the Personal Year (PY) 9 include travel, change of home and or job, and the making of new and exciting friendships, often accompanied by the termination of some older relationships we have since outgrown. It is also an excellent year for squaring old debts and extending the hand of peace to anyone with whom we might be at variance. A strong sense of humanitarian responsibility, tolerance and improved understanding will noticeably prevail during this year.

○ *Ruling 9 people* will be in no doubt as to the importance of this year, for they will feel its vibrant power in every action. It should be their year of notable success. As the crest of their cycle, it brings them to an increased level of personal responsibility and idealism in whatever humanitarian field they express themselves. Should they be already overly ambitious, this year will strengthen their enthusiasm for egocentric success and could incite them to a degree of recklessness that might lead to extremely painful lessons.

Fanaticism, superiority and excessive seriousness can detract the individual from enjoying the excitement of this dramatic year.

○ JANUARY IN PY9

Don't just talk about it, do it. To ensure that the enormous potential of this year is best utilised, commence it with a resolve to act on every suitable opportunity for positive change. Resist the tendency to merely talk about the exciting prospects for change (in travel, work, home, and so on), and commence positive steps this month to wisely plan them.

○ FEBRUARY IN PY9

When you feel it in your bones, move them and follow the feeling. Often we feel the need for change, but rationalise it away through lack of courage. We need to be more aware of our intuition – respect it by honouring our sensitivities, such as through music, meditation or in nature. Allow time for adequate relaxation to spiritually recharge.

○ MARCH IN PY9

Who is the boss, you or your ambitions? Ambitious projects will do very well this month, so long as they do not get out of control. It is an excellent month for overseas travel, especially to new and exotic locales. It is also ideal for the commencement of new studies – mental stimulation will always make life more exciting.

○ APRIL IN PY9

Continued financial success should accelerate this month, especially if your affairs have been efficiently organised and you are in control. It is also a powerful time for practical hobbies (such as gardening, carpentry, pottery, and so on) to take a surprisingly prominent role in your affairs.

○ MAY IN PY9

Pay special attention to your loved ones this month. In the euphoria of change and financial success, it is easy to take for granted those who are nearest and dearest to us. Take time to show appreciation to family and work associates – it will bring amazing awards to all, especially the giver.

○ JUNE IN PY9

New creative and artistic endeavours will excel under this vibration, but be serious about them. It is not a month for superficiality or half-heartedness. Travel again features strongly this month, especially for long journeys.

○ JULY IN PY9

Do it now month! This is the time to put into action any important changes you have been contemplating, but have so far failed to implement. It is a practical time when our understanding greatly benefits from wise actions.

○ AUGUST IN PY9

Financial independence should take a huge forward step this month, especially if you have implemented the creative concepts of recent months. Take care not to let your financial success detract from your emotional enjoyment of life; especially guard against any aloofness towards your loved ones.

○ SEPTEMBER IN PY9

The power of choice will be felt nowhere more strongly than during this month. You should feel intensified courage to start new projects or more fully develop those you are currently involved in. With perseverance, your timidity may be dispelled forever by your actions during this powerful month.

○ OCTOBER IN PY9

(From October 1, influence of next year's PY1 starts to rise, while this year's power starts to slowly diminish.) The focus this month is towards self-expression. It is a month of action, as your ability to adapt to the year's changes is strengthened.

○ NOVEMBER IN PY9

Increased confidence in your intuition will improve your decision-making abilities and increase the practical side of your idealism, bringing with it an enhanced level of success in your life both professionally and domestically.

○ DECEMBER IN PY9

This is the last of the three-month cusp, or change-over period, between PY9 and PY1, and its power is in mental acuity, strengthening your ability for understanding rather than persisting with habitual action. Recognise the need to evaluate demands placed on you so that you achieve a win-win situation for your efforts and are not led into futile alleys of negativity.

○ PERSONAL YEAR 1 — AN ACTIVE YEAR OF ADJUSTMENT

This is an extremely powerful doing year for personal growth and expression as we adjust to the changes wrought during the now-concluded PY9. The power of this year encourages us to dare to be different as we improve in self-confidence and extricate ourselves from the limitations religion-dominated society feels justified in inflicting upon its faithful. This is an excellent year for the breaking of old habits. Indeed, adaptation to a new lifestyle invariably demands such severance.

It is a especially powerful year for improving ourselves financially and for and selling on a wide scale, such as with real estate, business interests and investments. However, the most significant and permanent success will only be achieved when people's motives are genuinely for the common good, free of personal greed and recklessness.

○ *Ruling 10 people* will find adaptation so effortless this year that they can be easily lulled into an attitude of frivolity. They must be careful to avoid recklessness, especially in financial matters, and take heed not to succumb to egocentricity. With appropriate self-discipline, they will find it a year of significant material growth and personal popularity.

○ JANUARY IN PY1

The time is now. There is no time like this month to flow with the surge of change that carries over from last year. It is a powerful month for business growth and for personal assertiveness.

○ FEBRUARY IN PY1

Self-confidence will improve with the strengthening of your intuition. Take care to use time wisely, rather than flaunt it on egocentric diversions.

○ MARCH IN PY1

Think and grow rich. This is a powerful vibration for the development of lateral thinking, memory training and the solving of hitherto difficult problems. From this expanded mental perspective can emanate a new dimension to your prosperity consciousness.

○ April in PY1

A review month – one in which to tie loose ends, and consolidate the dynamic changes of the past months, and to review and organise future growth. It is intended to be an intensely practical month when balance and moderation should prevail.

○ May in PY1

It is never wise to be typecast. The excitement and joy of your new-found freedom will improve your confidence in self-expression, creating surprises for many who thought they knew you. Remember, people only know of us what they know of themselves – and for most, that is rather limiting.

○ June in PY1

Grasp whatever creative opportunities come your way this month. Be prepared for the development of a new aspect of your expression, be it artistic, domestic or financial. Focus on home is powerful this month, but ensure it is creative and progressive otherwise anxiety can creep in and upset your nerves.

○ July in PY1

This is a back-to-basics month, when theories and plans must give way to actions. Put your new concepts to the ultimate test, set them in motion, then be prepared to discard those parts that do not suit, recognising that we sometimes conceive more than we can effectively use.

○ August in PY1

A strong sense of independence flows this moth, but take care that it does not distance you from your family or work associates, for close cooperation is fundamental to your continuing success. Use you independence wisely and it will be a month of abundance.

○ SEPTEMBER IN PY1

New areas of responsibility, promotion or travel can bring significant change to your life this month. Understand that it is all a vital part of your growth, so take it calmly and avoid recklessness.

○ OCTOBER IN PY1

An important stabilising month in which to undertake those duties that are incomplete, or not yet initiated. Bring your affairs in order as preparation for the new emphasis due to enter your life next month, recognising that your power to adapt is at its peak this month.

○ NOVEMBER IN PY1

(From November 1, influence of next year's PY2 starts to rise, while this year's power starts to slowly diminish.) Satisfaction and enhanced self-esteem should greet your successes to date as the winds of change subside and a new spiritual reality starts to strengthen your intuition.

○ DECEMBER IN PY1

Your past year's emphasis on action now gives way to a quieter and deeper understanding as your feelings touch a new depth of personal awareness. Many missing pieces of the previous months' puzzles now fall into place to bring a more holistic understanding to your life.

PERSONAL YEAR 2 — A SPIRITUAL GROWTH YEAR OF SHARING

Though not with the power of a peak number, this is a year in which its own powerful nature can be significant enough to cause many a turbulent personality to embrace calmness. Spiritual development is the primary feature of this year with an enhanced awareness of life's more subtle qualities. Rather than being a year of major change, it is one in which the development of emotional control, spiritual awareness and accentuated intuition can be expected.

Central to the growth under this year's vibration is the need to actively develop the power of meditation. By this means, more than any other, the body's cellular alignment is restored to achieve the inner power we all want as our limitless energy reserve and our magnetic essence. By this means, we learn to be in command of our emotions, to act rather then react, to replace uncertainty and doubt with confidence and security, and to wisely discriminate between the more important and the less important aspects of our daily life.

Following the two previous years of progress, some people develop a tendency to rest on their laurels or lapse into complacency. It is then that negativity takes the opportunity to develop those reactive emotions of fear, nervousness, argumentativeness and insecurity that can sometimes manifest in the most unexpected ways to make an otherwise likeable person seem quite obnoxious or unbearably power-crazed. Realise it as a year for cooperation, for working together in one or more partnerships (home, work, sports, and so on). To satisfactorily achieve this, we need to be more loving and more accepting – further growth aspects of this year.

○ *Ruling 2 and Ruling 11 people* will be especially susceptible to the increased sensitivity accompanying this year's vibrations. It should not be surprising for them if their psychic awareness takes on a significantly elevated level of expression, almost projecting their consciousness into another dimension. Their cooperation with this development by allowing adequate time for meditation and spiritual studies will be powerfully beneficial for their own understanding of it's power, as well as for their role in guiding others.

○ January in PY2

A new level of spiritual awareness will be felt from the very beginning by those who allow themselves to become so attuned. Don't hesitate to express this new or enhanced power for in so doing its integrity will become the more speedily established as your spiritual confidence grows.

○ February in PY2

An intensified power of intuition is inherent in this month's vibrations and you should avail yourself of every appropriate opportunity for its expression, for this month is one in which cooperation and sharing feature strongly.

○ March in PY2

With the powerful mind vibrations of this month, it is important that your enhanced spiritual powers are understood and that you do not use them for manipulation or power-seeking. Undertaking a new course in spiritual growth will be highly beneficial this month.

○ April in PY2

Use it or lose it. No growth in spirituality or sensitivity is of any value unless it is applied to positive living. This is a month of action in which just such application could not be more appropriate.

○ May in PY2

For those who have wisely used the power of this year, an exhilarated freedom will enhance your new level of personal confidence. For those who have wasted their power so far, moodiness and frustration will indicate that you need to remedy the situation as you are already halfway through the year.

○ June in PY2

For those living positively, an expanded level of creative consciousness attends to your efforts, so you will find this a powerful month
to start a creative hobby or develop an existing one. For those who
have not yet come alive, worry, stress and a reactive nature will lead
you to almost certain illness.

○ July in PY2

Nature never forgives. Another month of rewards or penalties
should alert the slow learner to the fact that the winners in this life
are those who move with the opportunities. No greater insult can
be thrown at our Creator than to ignore repeated growth opportunities; no greater appreciation can our Creator receive than to witness the wise investment of time and energy into appropriate
opportunities that show up in our personal life.

○ August in PY2

This is a potent month of enhanced spiritual power in which our
independence and wisdom can attain new heights as we more fully
discover who we really are – beings far greater than we conceived
in our imagination. But this can only develop from applying our
power to wise action.

○ September in PY2

(From September 1, the influence of next year's PY3 starts to rise,
while this year's power now starts to slowly diminish.) Our idealism should not be satisfied with anything short of excellence as our
new enlightenment accepts no compromise in its enhanced richness. For those who have yet to achieve the full potential of the
PY2, the three months to the end of November should provide
ample opportunity.

○ OCTOBER IN PY2

This is an excellent month for improving finances if decisions are intuitively guided and we do not react to other people or external pressures that do not feel right.

○ NOVEMBER IN PY2

This is the month when final arrangements for securing the most desirable partnership should be completed, whether it be in business, love or any other aspect of your life. It is also a wise time to take whatever opportunity for relaxation comes your way.

○ DECEMBER IN PY2

Considerable power from next year's vibrations will already be making its presence felt as feelings of change and the desire for travel. It is an interesting transition month in which the diminishing spiritual growth unites with the emerging mental growth, providing double benefit to those who are ready to avail of such an opportunity.

○ PERSONAL YEAR 3 – A MIND EXPANSIVE YEAR

Between the peak PYNs and the trough of the PY4 comes this year of surprisingly intensified mental power that provides the appropriate rounded development for this portion of the Personal Year cycle. Under this vibration, our thinking and observing faculties are attuned to an acute peak of alertness. It is a year when the intellect thirsts for knowledge and expression. For some, it could involve study of an academic nature. Others might prefer to investigate life and its philosophies, while some might seek enlightenment through personal growth.

The usual means of mental expansion this year are either through an educational course or extensive travel. Whatever the choice, it is important to realise that this year is one in which the further development of memory is vital, for the 3 vibration is the gateway to the mind through memory.

We should always realise that memory is the foundation of self-esteem and self-confidence, as well as the bridge between our conscious and unconscious minds. The continual alertness and growing capacity of our memory is invariably distinguishable between the ageing and the ageless people.

On the lighter side of the PY3, we should recognise the need for balance by ensuring that time is allowed in our lives for humour, happy occasions, bright company and the appreciation of a good joke.

o *Ruling 3 people* will be especially attuned to this year's vibrations, but they must learn to control their high level of rationality to ensure that it does not swamp their feelings. For them, the enhanced mental alertness they will experience this year needs to be channelled into avenues of constructive and expansive awareness for their personal satisfaction and for the peace of mind of those with whom they associate (who may otherwise grow tired of an overbalanced mentality and become the subject of frequent destructive criticism).

o JANUARY IN PY3

The need for self-expression is stimulated this month as the mind seeks to have its newly-stimulated thoughts translated into active life. Many new plans are likely to be conceived and discussed this month and every effort should be made to act upon those that seem appropriate. Remember, this is a month for individual action.

○ FEBRUARY IN PY3

This is a powerful month for the intuitive faculties to guide the mental and provide that profound combination that easily accomplishes any challenge. Intuition should be all the more attuned after last year's spiritual progress.

○ MARCH IN PY3

Acuity of memory is at its peak with the double 3. Concepts will either take on new meaning or will be discarded, no longer relevent. This is a perfect month to commence a new course of study or undertake a new job training program.

○ APRIL IN PY3

The stabilising vibrations of this month provide an appropriate time for reflection and consolidation of the mind's growth thus far. It is also a month of action where and when appropriate.

○ MAY IN PY3

Exciting mental expansiveness brings with it a euphoria that sets the heart singing. It is especially a time for heightened thoughtfulness towards our loved ones, for they are sometimes omitted from our year of busy mental growth.

○ JUNE IN PY3

Even newer concepts develop under this creative 6 vibration. The new season brings with it an added dimension of enlightenment and some further growth in memory expansiveness. But this can be all negated if anxiety intervenes, as it sometimes does when positive creativity is swamped by worry.

○ July in PY3

Behind every mental experience is a philosophic understanding that is often overlooked in our headlong rush toward "progress." But to the true thinker, philosophic understanding is the foundation upon which further mental growth is enhanced. The vibrations of this month are most conducive to the development of this foundation.

○ August in PY3

The key to independence is lateral thinking, the mental exercise by which the exceptional departs from the conventional. If it is in you, but has yet to emerge, this month offers the right vibrations.

○ September in PY3

Another powerful mind month in which we come to terms with the added responsibility that comes with our expanded knowledge. But be especially mindful to find the joy amid life's seriousness.

○ October in PY3

(From October 1, the influence of next year's PY4 gradually begins, while this year's power will be felt to slowly diminish.) Mental growth unexpressed in action is little better than bland theory, so take this last powerful opportunity to apply the substance of your new concepts to your practical life to ensure they work for you.

○ November in PY3

This is a month of accentuated feelings when all our faculties – mental, spiritual and physical – combine for success. Ensure adequate relaxation and meditation periods.

○ DECEMBER IN PY3

In the final analysis, if a concept works to improve our lives and brings added joy, it is worth keeping. Otherwise, useless theories tend to clog our valuable brain cells.

○ PERSONAL YEAR 4 - A YEAR OF CONSOLIDATION

Physical and material factors dominate this trough year. Rest and stability are vital to the regenerate and consolidate the previous five years' development. It is a year of squaring (as symbolised geometrically by the four-sided figure), when everything is brought to a reckoning and the unwanted aspects eliminated, as a vine is pruned in winter to make way for the coming new growth the following spring.

This is an ideal year for integrating Basic Self (body and emotions) Conscious Self (thoughts and ideas) with High Self (the eternal soul). Those who do not follow the need for time out to relax and adjust could find themselves in a state of disharmony, leading to frustration, confusion and fear. Any attempt at major changes in affairs or lifestyles during this year are rarely successful, leading instead to material loss in either finances, health or both.

People who are usually regarded as being highly strung, whose nerves are ever tense and whose sensitivities are acute, should be especially careful to avoid any disharmony in their dealings with others this year. For them, a relaxed vacation will be most beneficial.

○ *Ruling 4 people* cannot be blamed for feeling quite frustrated under this year's vibrations. Invariably, they will fail to recognise it as a year of consolidation, trying instead to maintain the impetus of the progress achieved during the previous four years. As a result, their nerves take a severe battering. For them, increased rest and reduced emotional disturbances (such as avoiding TV, movie "thrillers," and domestic or work arguments) will help reduce the toll on their health. The inclusion in their diet of adequate B-complex vitamins will be of enormous help in restoring nerve energy, as will appropriate homoeopathic nerve tonics; but addictive tranquilliser drugs should be avoided for they only incite secondary problems.

Ruling 22/4 people should accept the same advice, but with the additional suggestion that they recognise their more spiritual essence and organise their daily routines to permit periods for meditation and relaxation. Additional spiritual nourishment for them includes time to read appropriate spiritual books, listen to harmonious music or, more ideally, become involved in creating music or writing books aided by their powerful intuition.

○ JANUARY IN PY4

Dare to be different. Be courageous as you confront your choices and eliminate unneeded matter and acquaintances from your affairs. Be confident and firm in your convictions. Your sensitivities are vulnerable this month, so focus them on your loved ones and consolidate these relationships.

○ FEBRUARY IN PY4

Do not let people intimidate you into doing what you prefer to avoid. Be confident and firm in your convictions. Your sensitivities are vulnerable this month, so focus them on your loved ones and consolidate these relationships.

○ MARCH IN PY4

Understand your needs as opposed to your wants. Seek not those things outside you, for you have it all within. Avoid wasting time on distant fancies, recognising that we rarely use a fraction of our potential because we take insufficient time to understand it. The vibrations of this month are particularly conducive for reversing that habit.

○ APRIL IN PY4

If you do not accept the need to consolidate, this can be a particularly trying month in which your nerves are tried almost to their limit. Many people experience unusual sicknesses under this vibration, but they will doubtless be nerve-oriented. Rest and remedial nourishment will provide the.

○ MAY IN PY4

Discover the freedom of detaching from old, limiting habits, both at home and at work. Take time to relax on a restful vacation to avoid nerve damage. Free yourself of unwanted "baggage," such as clothes you will no longer wear, books you will not again read and useless furniture – others can use them.

○ JUNE IN PY4

Your creative side can now be used to advantage to develop new and more efficient techniques for doing those things you have been avoiding or have been doing routinely and without thinking for so long. Take care not to allow worry or anxiety to cloud your actions. Realising that you can only live in the present, so concentrate on what you are doing instead of thinking about something else to be done later.

○ JULY IN PY4

This can be another difficult month for those who are not prepared to consolidate and conserve their energies. For them, it will be remembered as a month of loss; but realise that these are necessary sacrifices to show us when we are being too stubborn. For those with a deeper understanding, this can be a month of philosophic enlightenment as they undertake further mental and physical "house cleaning."

○ AUGUST IN PY4

If our year to date has been one of successful consolidation, this month will bring rewards of a new dimension in personal independence and wisdom. Otherwise, we will feel aloof and perhaps "turned off" from our loved ones.

○ SEPTEMBER IN PY4

Take care not to be tempted to become overly ambitious under this vibration, for it is more one of responsibility, preparing the way for the coming mini-peak. This is an excellent month for that well-earned restful vacation.

○ OCTOBER IN PY4

A month of compounded physical vibrations, this is an excellent period to start a suitable program to get the body into its optimum shape and fitness. Seek to finish your house cleaning, at home and office, giving away all unneeded and unused items. Make way for the new in all aspects of your life.

○ NOVEMBER IN PY4

(From November 1, the influence of next year's PY5 starts to be felt, while this year's power starts to diminish.) You should feel a new freedom, a lightness and happiness, your sensitivity more acute as you begin to reap the benefits of the declining stabilising year. If you succumbed to the nerve problems during the year, you could still be feeling ill at ease until you accept the remedies as previously offered.

○ DECEMBER IN PY4

You should now understand so much more about yourself and life, but do not get too enthusiastic in your planning for next year until this vibration is fully exhausted, for it is still the consolidating PY4 and this month is your last chance to really get to know its benefits as a foundation for the coming years of growth.

○ PERSONAL YEAR 5 — A YEAR OF FREEDOM

Spiritual and emotional factors prevail this year. Its vibrations span the gap between last year's trough and next year's creative mini-peak, igniting the power of freedom, generated by heightened psychic awareness and personal expression. This leads to the development of our talents to find release from material and social confinement, replacing them with a new focus on artistic expression, whether for a hobby or professionally. Some have launched the basis for a new career under this vibration. Others have discovered their freedom in a change of home, moving to the country and away from city confinement.

Ruling 5 people will find this a year in which their desires for freedom become almost obsessive. However, they must realise that it is not always physical freedom they need, though it is sometimes easier to believe so, thereby rationalising and masking an emptiness in personal understanding. Their primary need is for freedom of expression, a quality that is comparatively new to human life but, thankfully, becoming more and more universal. This expression can best be achieved through the arts, for it is soon realised that to express ourselves freely demands far more than just words. Music, painting, pottery or any similar form of artistic expression provide the vent for our sensitivity and much needed nourishment for the nerves, helping us to develop that all-important personal calmness.

○ JANUARY IN PY5

A new and revitalised personal assertiveness will often surprise family and friends, yet seem natural and normal to you under this vibration. Feel the freedom of its expression in your daily life.

○ FEBRUARY IN PY5

Heightened intuitive and spiritual awareness can open new depths of understanding and expression this month, bringing with it the desire for increased peace and harmony. This is an excellent month to begin study in personal growth or any of the metaphysical sciences.

○ MARCH IN PY5

With the increase in personal confidence engendered by an enriched freedom of expression, you find it easier to put your plans into action and gain improved satisfaction from a new sense of achievement, thereby resisting any tendency toward old lazy habits.

○ APRIL IN PY5

Ensure that whatever you plan has a solid foundation, and have the confidence to throw off unwanted restraints, especially with regard to work and study. Spend as much time as possible in the quiet of the country – there is no better nourishment for your nerves.

○ MAY IN PY5

To relocate home and or work away from the hustle and bustle of the city will be a compelling force, from now for most of the year, as you seek to expand your need for freedom. Love will feature strongly under this month's vibrations (and for the next few months) – allow yourself to both express and receive it.

○ June in PY5

This is an excellent month in which to develop a creative hobby. For many, it becomes a powerful month for buying or selling a home, especially if you plan to move somewhere with more space. Buying an older home to revitalise or restore provides a most lucrative hobby.

○ July in PY5

Do it now. What you have been planning or talking about, but have not yet put into action, now stands before you as a challenge. This is an excellent month for learning through action.

○ August in PY5

Settle the inner conflicts that might exist early in this month by acting on your intuition, rather than reacting to support your prejudices. Allow your wisdom to flourish through the courage of your actions, correcting anything in you life that does not seem worthy to you.

○ September in PY5

(From September 1, the influence of next year's PY6 starts to be felt, while this year's power slowly starts to wane.) An enhanced level of understanding provides new confidence, inspiring you to take more responsibility for positive action. No longer will you allow others to determine what is best for you – you are aware of the ultimate ideals, needing only to enact them.

○ October in PY5

A month of action encourages you to pursue those ideals considered last month, or to intensify those you commenced in July. Don't pass up another golden opportunity to see your new freedom of expression reach physical maturity.

○ November in PY5

Many of the new avenues of thought and metaphysical contemplation you have been considering this past year are now ready to test. If you have not already done so, apply them to your life and feel your freedom expand and your intuition become all the keener.

○ December in PY5

And now the understanding of what this year has been all about becomes so much clearer. You realise that love does not mean dependency, that freedom does not mean abandonment or laziness, that self-confidence does not mean boastfulness. At last, you have learned that the meaning of temperance is balance in all things suitable and avoidance of that which is undesirable.

○ Personal Year 6 — A year of creativity

This is the year of the mini-peak, its focus on accumulation of power that seeks vent through one's investment in creative time. New creative projects undertaken this year will have the most favourable aspects for success, especially if their underlying principle is directed toward the upliftment of humankind. It is a year in which the formation of any worthwhile business undertaking will considerably benefit.

It is also a year of focus on the home and on personal relationships. Creative activities related to the home will receive a significant boost under this vibration. In the area of relationships, many are either secured or released as underlying integrity casts free any falseness or negativity. Persisting with such undesirable traits will ensure that this is a most difficult year, inciting intense anxiety, arguments and hatred.

Clearly, the lesson of this year is to come to terms with facts as they are. It's also important to recognise what it is to have personal honesty and integrity, and a positive attitude. Then it will be a most rewarding year, crowned by happiness, creative achievement and sound financial success.

○ *Ruling 6 people* are the most tested under this vibration, for the intensification of their creativity and personal integrity combine to make it a powerful, yet cleansing period. Those engaged in the positive aspects of the 6 will find their creativity boosted as they attain a new high in happiness. They would have it no other way. Though there are many Ruling 6s that have not yet seen the light, preferring to dwell in the mud-hole of negativity, adopting worry and anxiety as their trademarks. They are already sick and will only become sicker as their bodies become more enervated and their attitude to life leads to further loneliness. Adopting the positive, creative approach is their only answer.

○ JANUARY IN PY6

Talk is cheap! This is a testing month for your newly acquired sense of balance (temperance), to test your resolve for acting on your creativity rather than verbally entertaining it. Do not allow climatic extremes or unbalanced physical desires to detract from your creative plans. Remember that one of the vital aspects of creativity is its power for adaptability.

○ FEBRUARY IN PY6

Respond to the increasing surge of excitement as you discover a new depth of meaning to your feelings. Do not be timid to express them, whether it be in personal, social or business affairs.

○ MARCH IN PY6

Realise the impossible dream. This is an especially powerful period for worthy business and commercial pursuits – from the beginning of the month until the end of September this year. Be confident in your affirmations and plan for the "possible dream."

○ APRIL IN PY6

Act upon your plans with the confidence of Alexander the Great, but with more temperance. (He died from gastronomic excesses just prior to this 33rd birthday. He had already conquered half the world but had failed to conquer his stomach!) This is a month for powerful, well-organised action and financial abundance.

○ MAY IN PY6

Confidence increases with success, but take care not to let the ego run riot. Maintain sensitivity to your feelings and wise compassion in your relationships.

○ JUNE IN PY6

Not even the sky is a limit! This is the peak month of the year when you powers of innovation and originality know no bounds. Home, business and social affairs will be amazingly enhanced in direct proportion to your positive outlook. The money can surely flow this month, so let it happen.

○ JULY IN PY6

Come back to earth. Stabilise and secure the great advances of this year. It's as though you are assimilating the vast input to your biocomputer (your brain) acquired so far in your PY6. Organise to tie any loose ends and secure any floating foundations before you make your next foray.

○ August in PY6

The power of this month lies in its unique combination of creative growth and personal independence. Resultant from this combination is a degree of wisdom far superior to any experienced to date. But it is only accessible to those positive people who shun the opposite. Negative people will tend to feel detached, unloved and badly done by – only they can alter that.

○ September in PY6

For those open to progress and excitement, this will be a powerful month of change, most likely involving travel andor job promotion. Financial aspects are also excellent, but remember that optimum success attends only those who embrace a positive attitude.

○ October in PY6

(From October 1, the influence of next year's PY7 will slowly begin and slow our progress as this year's power gradually wanes.) It is a month of individual growth in which we should be thoroughly clear as to what we want and how we seek to achieve it. Preciseness, even in our thoughts, avoids confusion, discursiveness and delays. This is important as the year's power starts to wane in preparation for the following consolidation. It is an abundant month for finalising buying and selling details.

○ November in PY6

Your intuition is your ever-faithful guide and this month is attuned to preparing you for some significant lifestyle changes as the dynamic year just concluding abdicates its power to the approaching consolidating trough of PY7.

○ DECEMBER IN PY6

It is imperative that you understand the changes now occurring and be alert to adjusting to the most significant transition in the Personal Year Cycle, as will be observed from the graph on page 133. It is a time for slowing down and creative evaluation.

○ PERSONAL YEAR 7 – A TROUGH YEAR OF FOCUS

Similar to the PY4, this is a trough year of consolidation when no major change should be undertaken. However, it is a highly significant year in which we learn to intensely focus on previous years' growth with a view to better understand our life. As such, it is a vital year for learning through personal experience. For many, this implies sacrifice brought about by a failure to recognise and apply guidance from the higher powers and their own natural wisdom. When we live in thoughtless reaction, we expose ourselves to the need for firm corrective measures – prompt karma we might call it. Such sacrifices invariably result in the loss of money, health and or love. They always have purpose, for they are designed to awaken and return us to the Path.

It is wise to avoid any major changes in financial or domestic affairs during this year, for it is a period of stabilisation, as opposed to expansion, of pruning dead wood to make way for the new growth of the ensuring years. It is also a powerful teaching/sharing year in which frequent opportunities present themselves for guiding others toward our level of understanding.

○ *Ruling 7 people* will often suffer seemingly severe hardships under this vibration. But their experience will invariably appear far worse to the outsider. These people are not unfamiliar with sacrifice, for this is their established pattern of learning. And it will continue to be that way until they attain a sufficient degree of personal awareness and wisdom. Once this is achieved, they

become excellent teachers, practical philosophers and helpers to humankind, thereby fulfilling the purpose intended by their Ruling Number.

○ JANUARY IN PY7

This can be a difficult month of adjustment for those who have become addicted to continual progress. But we all must learn to accept the things we cannot change, and this is an irrevocable year of consolidation. If it be in disagreement with your wants, then examine them and act wisely, or this could become a year of significant loss for you.

○ FEBRUARY IN PY7

If you have not yet succeeded in accepting the need to focus on stabilising this year, then quieten your mind and body, turn inward and rely on your intuition for guidance. Take time to embrace periods of silence and meditate whenever possible. Be especially attentive to stabilising your love life.

○ MARCH IN PY7

Your level of personal understanding is strengthened during this month when the mind number 3 prevails. Things become clearer and your life becomes more readily understood, unless you refuse to accept the inevitable and choose instead to play the role of the victim.

○ APRIL IN PY7

Those who have refused to slow down and consolidate can expect this to be a month of material sacrifice – financially and, perhaps, in health. How else will the universe teach you? Ideally, it is a month for practical organising and for discarding unwanted aspects of life.

○ MAY IN PY7

Focus on stabilising your love life this month, not only with your partner but also with your children and or close family. Be more free with them in your personal expression – let them see how loving you really are.

○ JUNE IN PY7

When one door closes, look for the one (or maybe two) that opens. But don't rush in (leave that to the fools). Develop a creative patience, take your time and consider all aspects before making your move, for the best might be somewhat camouflaged yet worthy of investigation.

○ JULY IN PY7

Many things you have been reluctant to surrender until now could become forfeited as your path is cleared of limitations to your growth. The loss will hurt, but the sacrifices are worth it. If the opportunity for teaching occurs, throw yourself into it with enthusiasm and be prepared for success.

○ AUGUST IN PY7

(From August 1, the influence of next year's PY8 starts to slowly strengthen, while this year's power starts to wane.) Now you begin to understand the reasons for those sacrifices, if you have not already. Your philosophic awareness has brought you much wisdom to employ in sound decision-making when it comes to shaping your independence.

○ SEPTEMBER IN PY7

Change is in the air. You can feel life become lighter as a new-found wisdom re-energises your confidence. Your life will respond with improved happiness, peace and security. But if you continue to fight your High Self, sacrifices will certainly continue.

○ OCTOBER IN PY7

An enhanced self-confidence attends your efforts as your finances and health improve, so long as you have thoroughly surrendered all unwanted baggage on your journey along the Path.

○ NOVEMBER IN PY7

With greater confidence in your intuition, your wise decisions attract improved results as you grow in independence. If only you could have achieved this level of understanding without all that sacrifice, Maybe you will remember for the next cycle eight years from now.

○ DECEMBER IN PY8

Plans should now be afoot to develop new ideas, some of which you have been patiently contemplating since June. Go for it! A great year is coming up and leading into a powerful growth cycle.

○ PERSONAL YEAR 8 – A YEAR OF INDEPENDENCE
AND WISDOM

This is a year of rapid change as we emerge from a consolidating trough onto the steep rise toward our next peak and the start of a new cycle of growth and prosperity. Many new opportunities manifest under this vibration as we assert our independence with growing wisdom. For some, it will be in the form of a significant improvement in their financial affairs. For the majority, there will emerge a heightened spiritual independence in which they recognise how much emotional control and understanding they have achieved and how much more emphasis they now place on living (acting), rather than existing (reacting).

○ *Ruling 8 people* have already acquired an appreciable measure of independence and wisdom to the extent that their living has been positive. Otherwise, they will have built around themselves an isolating wall, confusing aloofness with independence and experiencing difficulties in communicating with their close associates, whom they so often take for granted.

○ JANUARY IN PY8

New financial benefits will flow this month, as will abundant new ideas. Learn to express these ideas to those who might be interested with them to encourage essential feedback. This provides an excellent opportunity for evaluation so long as your ego does not intrude by identifying with the ideas.

○ FEBRUARY IN PY8

Your intuition is especially poignant this month, but it only becomes of value when acted upon. So many opportunities will avail themselves that your intuitive guidance is needed to distinguish what are the most important to you now. It is also a powerful month for the strengthening of partnerships, both in love and commerce.

○ MARCH IN PY8

Guided by your intuition, you are more able to analyse and understand what is best from the many options now prevalent in your life. It is also a month in which your enjoyment of life finds a new high. Have fun with it!

○ APRIL IN PY8

A powerful financial period starts this month. If you act with wisdom, it will set a highly profitable tone for the next few years. But be sure to allow time in your busy schedule for loved ones.

○ MAY IN PY8

A strong sense of freedom prevails this month, bringing with it many changes in your outlook. Endeavour to take every opportunity to enjoy your life, though you will probably be torn between commercial pre-occupation and domestic desires. It is highly desirable to have a balance of the two.

○ JUNE IN PY8

Creative new business opportunities develop very well under this month's power. It is also a month when the home features strongly, so give your domestic creativity every opportunity to express itself. It is a powerful month for buying or selling your home.

○ JULY IN PY8

This is very much an action month of strong ethical substance. Do not try any tricks this month for they will surely be to your detriment. If your actions cannot stand the test of openness and honesty, it is best to abort them.

○ AUGUST IN PY8

Exciting opportunities will present themselves for your enhanced financial independence, as this is a very powerful month for money matters. Again, be careful not to allow yourself to be swamped with work, overlooking time to be spent at home and with loved ones.

○ SEPTEMBER IN PY8

(From September 1, the influence of next year's PY9 peak starts to become apparent, while this year's power starts to decline.) Your strong ideals will stand you in good stead for continued financial success, with responsibility on the home front becoming even stronger. It is also a month offering strong prospects for overseas travel.

○ OCTOBER IN PY8

This is another powerful month for profitable buying and selling. As the changes begin to take effect in the transition toward the coming PY9, adaptability assumes an increasingly important role as a personal characteristic and this month enhances its power.

○ NOVEMBER IN PY8

Personal sensitivity can push your awareness to new heights, or it can cause you to hide behind a wall of isolation if you have not yet come to full terms with your abundance and positive outlook. Take time to relax, meditate and spend time in nature as an important counterbalance to a most progressive year to date.

○ DECEMBER IN PY8

New ideas will dance before your eyes this month, offering many opportunities for personal growth as the transition between the PY8 and PY9 occurs. Many of these ideas will be strikingly right-brained, so be prepared for surprises.

****

The foregoing offers general guidelines to understanding the Personal Years on a month-by-month basis. Obviously, not everyone will incur the same nature and degree of change each month, or we would all be like migrating birds or the performing animals that are trained to dance to the same tune in the same way. Hence, the breadth of description for each month is intended to provide an indication of the range of activities to be expected.

Between each Personal Year Number lies the cusp, or changeover period. This has a duration from two to five months, depending on the time of year in which the power of the existing PYN gradually resides, while that of the forthcoming PYN gradually develops dates of commencement of the cusp are not rigid. Though they are fairly reliable in the majority of lives, powerful environmental factors at times exert modifications beyond the control of the individual. Below the general dates of the start of the transition are indicated for each PYN and the duration of each PY, being either 13 or 10 months, is also shown.

- PY9 TO PY1 – OCTOBER 1; PY9 DURATION OF 13 MONTHS
- PY1 TO PY2 – NOVEMBER 1; PY1 DURATION OF 13 MONTHS
- PY2 TO PY3 – SEPTEMBER 1; PY2 DURATION OF 10 MONTHS
- PY3 TO PY4 – OCTOBER 1; PY3 DURATION OF 13 MONTHS
- PY4 TO PY5 – NOVEMBER 1; PY4 DURATION OF 13 MONTHS
- PY5 TO PY6 – SEPTEMBER 1; PY5 DURATION OF 10 MONTHS
- PY6 TO PY7 – OCTOBER 1; PY6 DURATION OF 13 MONTHS
- PY7 TO PY8 – AUGUST 1; PY7 DURATION OF 10 MONTHS
- PY8 TO PY9 – SEPTEMBER 1; PY8 DURATION OF 13 MONTHS

CHAPTER .10

The three phases of life - your "road map"

*T*o chart a journey into the unknown, a map is required. Yet the most unknown of journeys is what we call life. And where is our map? Did the planning genius, the Creator, desert us in this, our greatest need? Indeed not!

Though no one can be certain what might occur next in our lives, there is a "map" by which we can gain remarkable insight so long as our vehicle (the body) maintains its ability to take us there. It is true that no one can be certain of exactly what might occur in their lives tomorrow, or during the remainder of today for that matter. Most of us have varying types of plans or desires, but not until the moment is with us or has past can we be certain of what occurred. Even then, many people remain uncertain during or after the event, so unaware are they of what is transpiring in their lives.

This "map" of our journey is in three consecutive segments. It starts with our birth and is based on that only permanent aspect of our lives, our date of birth, the day on which we started our journey of individuality. However, unlike all other maps, this one has the unique quality of offering no final page. It just keeps expanding so long as we are prepared to keep progressing.

These three segments are known as adolescence, maturity and fulfilment. And provided that no karmic or environmental influences decree otherwise, our life will successfully encompass all three phases.

The initial phase, adolescence, starts at birth and prevails through the many changes in bodily development that take it to physical maturity. At a predetermined age, it gives way to the start of the second phase maturity. This period of adolescence witnesses the ongoing development of our physical body, assuming that karmic and environmental factors do not create a fatal change.

To students of metaphysics, it is no secret that certain external factors can be instrumental in terminating life during its early years, prior to reaching maturity. If this be the plan, the purpose for that life is comparatively simple and fulfilled early. Fortunately, such a destiny has always been in the minority and is becoming even more rare. With average life expectancy now around its highest in the history of humanity, we can more comfortably look to our life developing well into its third phase.

During the phase of adolescence, human lives are primarily concerned with physical experience. Even though their Personal Growth Cycles indicate varying degrees of influence of a spiritual or mental nature in certain years, the overriding emphasis is essentially physical. It is through the five physical senses that juveniles become attuned to life, are disciplined, recognise their relationship to and respect for their parents and the environment, attend school, and gain some measure of insight into an understanding of their individuality. Throughout their school years, young humans become heavily focused on the physical aspects of life – their own bodies and the bodies of others. The deceleration of physical growth in the latter teenage years is usually succeeded by accelerated mental and emotional activity. This is a period of many hurts and many triumphs, but it brings people to the threshold of real maturity when the physical playground is not longer the sole centre of attraction.

As they develop better self-possession of their emotions, and their mind starts to significantly expand its awareness, the person is found to be moving from adolescence to maturity, from the first to the second phase of their life. This transition occurs at the age at which they reach the first peak Pyramid, as discussed in the next chapter. Chronologically, this will be shown to be as young as twenty five, or as old as thirty four. Its duration of the second phase is of twenty seven years, three cycles each of the nine Personal Years.

Essentially a period of mental activity, the development of this second phase of human life is directed toward personal emotional control, the understanding of life, attaining financial security and the development of the family unit. Strong cyclic influences of varying physical and spiritual activity will continue to prevail during this phase, with the physical gradually losing its dominance while the spiritual gradually intensifies. Career development and financial independence are more easily achieved during this phase than any other, with myriad opportunities being presented as we pass through the diverse cycles of the Pyramids.

Maturity is a vital phase in the discovery of one's inner self, for the degree of success we achieve during these twenty seven years of stability will be instrumental in preparing us for the development of our third phase of life, our years of fulfilment.

From the year on which we reach the fourth peak of our Pyramids, our emphasis in growth takes on the primary focus of the spiritual. From financial independence, we graduate to the development of spiritual independence and the acquiring of wisdom far more profound than anything we have previously known. Any major changes in our financial or professional world should have been undertaken during the years of maturity, for rarely do radical changes transpire with success during the years of fulfilment. Modifications to our lifestyle can always be undertaken with wisdom, but if a radical change is contemplated in this third phase of life, extreme care must be taken.

Discovering the inner self takes on a whole new depth of meaning as we enter the astonishing world of spiritual awareness that awaits the mature person. Intuition, compassion, emotional expression, wisdom and a closer affinity with the "Creator" take on a degree of increasing development that knows no cessation so long as we seek to continue growing. And this is the crucial point!

Most people have an unconscious inner program about dying: they believe they will do so before they reach a three-figure age. Few people in middle life or younger seem able to contemplate living beyond 100 years of age. Even fewer older people are prepared to mentally make such a commitment. Just where this fallacious concept arose will be examined and negated in Chapter 16. We stay in the fulfilment phase until we finally depart from the body.

That this third phase of life should be our most rewarding is beyond question. After growing, training, investing and developing for over half a century, surely we deserve the reward of peaceful, joyous development of the inner self as awaits us for as long as we want to partake of it? And the most exciting aspect of all is that we actually have the choice. This is our real independence, the ultimate discovery of the inner self.

CHAPTER .11

The Pyramids – your peak connections of maturity

*P*yramid building started in Atlantis, migrated east and west, inspired kings, priests and the magi for millennia, and gave rise to this unique form of architecture that, even today, is emulated in the design of certain hotels and other public buildings. Central and South America, as well as Egypt, are home to extant pyramids to which millions of tourists make pilgrimage every year. What is so very special about this form of construction?

Evidence suggests that when Pythagoras studied in Egypt for twenty two years in the early sixth century BC, he came to understand the nature and purpose of those gigantic, peaked structures that were so highly revered by his mentors, the priests. Years later, when he was to formulate his profound teachings on life, Pythagoras reverted to these same pyramids as symbols of maturity.

To the ancient masters, pyramids had profound significance. Symbolically, they represented the human's aspirations toward their Creator and to ultimate perfection. Materially, they were constructed to attract and focus enormous power, as well as to perpetuate the secrets of eternal life. The total construction was not meant to be merely an impressive funereal edifice. It was instead a gigantic power source within which the knowledge and wisdom of the buried leaders could be amplified and then spiritually transmitted throughout the nation, thereby perpetuating their omniscient influence over the affairs of the people.

The mode of construction of the pyramids also involved the ancient mysteries, many of which remain undiscovered even today. But what we do know is that the ancient symbolism, as represented by these noble structures, has been adapted by Pythagoras, in consequence of his deep studies, to be representative of the other most noble structures, the human body in its maturing state.

Four Pyramids are constructed to represent human life through the years of maturity. These represent a period of 27 years, comprising three cycles, each of nine years. The age at which each person commences their ascent of the Pyramids is found by deducting their Ruling Number from the mystical number, 36. This number had a special significance in the design and construction of the ancient pyramids, representing as it does the square of 6, the number of creation. It also has a special significance for Biblical scholars, for it is the number of chapters of the fourth Book of the Bible – the name of which is *Numbers*.

By using the number 36, we are always assured of each person reaching their Pyramid Peaks in their Personal Year of 9, the year of change. Not by chance do these profound eventualities occur!

To illustrate the construction of the Pyramids for human birth dates, the following step-by-step method is offered. It is the simplest and most reliable means to learn the construction, so readers should be prepared to follow it precisely and to practise it on the birth dates of every person they can. For convenience, I have chosen the birth date of Queen Elizabeth II – April 21, 1926 – as the example:

○ STEP 1

Reduce the birth date to single digits for each of the three factors – month, day, year – ensuring that they are kept separate. Then place them in order as just described, the month placed first because it has the least strength of the three numbers. Thus, the month in our example is 4, the day is reduced to 3 (2 + 1 = 3) and the year is reduced to 9 (1 + 9 + 2 + 6 = 18; 1 + 8 = 9). The three numbers are then set out as follows, forming the base numbers upon which the Pyramids are to be constructed:

$$4 \quad 3 \quad 9$$

○ STEP 2

Build the first Pyramid based on the first two numbers as follows:

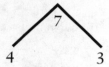

The Peak Number for this Pyramid is found by adding together the two numbers at the base of the Pyramid and, if necessary, resolving them to a single digit. But in this example it is already a single digit – 7 is therefore placed inside the first Peak unchanged. (If the base numbers were 7 and 8, the Peak Number would be 6, the total of 7 and 8 resolved to a single digit.)

○ STEP 3

Build the second Pyramid on the second and third base numbers:

The Peak Number for this second Pyramid is found by adding 3 and 9, the numbers at the base. These total 12, which has to be resolved to a single digit by adding 1 and 2. Thus, the Peak Number for the second Pyramid is 3.

○ STEP 4

Build the third Pyramid on the two existing Pyramids:

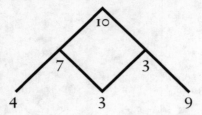

The Peak Number of the third Pyramid is the total of the first and second Peak Numbers. This is also resolved to a single digit, except if the total is 10 or 11 in which it remains as these full numbers. Our example shows that the Queen's third Peak Number is 10.

○ STEP 5

The final Pyramid is built around the other three because its base numbers are the first and third – 4 and 9 in this example:

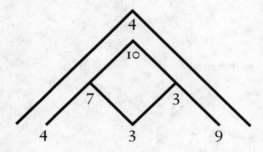

The Peak Number for this fourth Pyramid is the total of its two base numbers, 4 and 9, being 13. As with the other Peaks, this is resolved to a single digit, resulting in a Peak Number of 4; but if the total were 10 or 11 they would not be reduced. It is important to note that these two double numbers are only used if they appear on the third or fourth Peaks, for here their stronger spiritual influence has special importance as the third phase of life is approached.

○ STEP 6

We now have four Pyramids, representing the Queen's second stage of life – maturity. The Peak of each Pyramid indicates very important years in the period of the Queen's maturity. The age at which she reaches the first Peak is the chronological age at which her second stage of life (maturity) begins. This is found by deducting her Ruling Number, 7, from 36. Thus the age of 29 is placed adjacent to the first peak, together with the year at which this age is reached, viz. 1955.

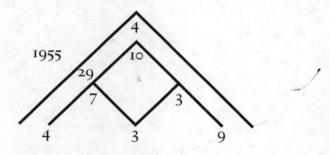

The ages attained at the remaining Pyramid peaks advance in nine-year intervals. Thus, the second peak is reached at age 38 in the year 1964; the third peak at age 47 in 1973; the fourth peak at age 56 in 1982. When these numbers are placed on the Pyramid diagram, it is completed as follows:

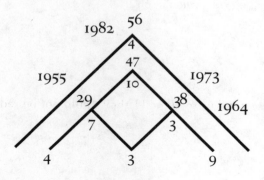

As an exercise to ensure you completely understand this important method, take a large piece of paper and write on it the birth date of Prince Philip – June 10, 1921. Now close the book and set up the diagram of his Pyramids; then check to see how much you have learned.

The complete Birth Chart and the Pyramids for Prince Philip is:

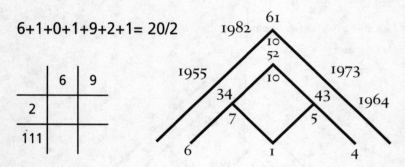

$$6+1+0+1+9+2+1= 20/2$$

If your efforts did not result in an identical diagram, it is suggested that you recheck your methods step by step. It is important that these methods be thoroughly understood before further progress can be made.

We must also be certain of the year that each Pyramid starts and the ages at which people of each Ruling Number arrive at their Peaks. The following chart illustrates this for those who do not wish to do their own calculation:

Ruling Number of person	Age at first peak	Age at second peak	Age at third peak	Age at fourth peak
2	34	43	52	61
3	33	42	51	60
4	32	41	50	59
5	31	40	49	58
6	30	39	48	57
7	29	38	47	56
8	28	37	46	55
9	27	36	45	54
10	26	35	44	53
11	25	34	43	52
22/4	32	41	50	59

Now that we are familiar with the setting up of the Pyramids, let us learn what they have to teach us. The most important set of numbers to be considered are the four Peak Numbers on the Pyramids.

○ THE PEAK NUMBERS

Due to the contrasting conditions necessary for each of us to achieve a well-balanced maturity, we need additional help to that normally available from the Ruling Number. We get our supplementary support from the four Peak Numbers on our Pyramids. The object of the Peak Numbers is to provide a valuable source of additional thrust at specific periods during the maturing years. For all who have karmically evolved beyond the barbarian stage (as has every thinking person), these numbers exert a special influence that starts toward the end of the year prior to the Peak Year (Personal Year 8) and rises to its acme of strength during the Peak

Year (Personal Year 9). This influence can be sustained for up to four years, significantly diminishing toward the close of the Personal Year 3 following the Peak Year.

○ **PEAK NUMBER** 1 will only be found on either (occasionally on both) the first or the second Pyramids. On the third or the fourth Pyramids, it becomes a 10. The 1 is an intensely practical number indicating that a period of individual effort is about to prevail, a period of definite personal expression. For most it will mean separation from previous involvements in which some degree of disharmony was inhibiting personal development, such as in marriage, business associations or social intercourse. You may be assured that no marriage, business relationship or friendship is severed unless it has already served its purpose. Some people will choose to avoid such separations with all possible effort, preferring to maintain the status quo. Notwithstanding, they will doubtless recognise a change in the nature of the relationship because they begin to exert more of their own individuality and become more expressive. The more spiritually advanced they are (in other words, the older the soul), the more they will exert their individuality this year and henceforth. The direction of their activities is usually consistent with their Ruling Number; the manner in which they express themselves will depend on their personality strengths indicated by their Birth Chart.

○ **PEAK NUMBER** 2 introduces a period when stronger spiritual values emerge. Lifestyle and habits will subtly embrace either a more intuitive or a more emotional manner. Whether the spiritual emphasis manifests as an improved state of awareness (its positive, most constructive form) or as a state of heightened emotions (its reactive and defeating form), will depend on the level of maturity thus far achieved. Obviously intuitive ability cannot be expected to develop if the individual is held captive by emotion. This is usually a period of hard work and slow progress in material affairs, but we cannot have it both ways. Remember, there is a right time for everything and one of the most important applications of numerology is to learn what our needs are and the right way, as well as the right time, to deal with them. To enforce material progress when under the influence of the Peak Number 2 would be to invite frustration, conflict and emotional enervation.

○ **PEAK NUMBER 3** is always a period when the emphasis should be directed toward intellectual pursuits. It is an important period of learning, of reviewing and analysing. Many people find the urge for travel particularly accentuated under the guidance of this vibration. At this period in their lives travel for such people assumes a very important role as a means of learning and expanding their insight into life. If they do not allow their mental faculties scope for positive expansion, they run the risk of becoming destructively critical, exacting and, not surprisingly, quite unpopular.

○ **PEAK NUMBER 4** brings with it increased material power. This might be expressed in any number of ways, depending upon the general level of maturity, Ruling Number and Birth Chart characteristics. For those people who are prepared for hard work, much can be achieved under this vibration. For those who need to acquire additional knowledge in dealing with the sense faculties to round off their maturitym and who are prepared to involve themselves in physical work, vital development will reward their efforts. But those who become overly ambitious, mercenary or covetous will find this period one of loss, rather than gain. Even though they might work harder, they will make no discernible progress while their motives are so egocentric. This can lead to a serious strain on their nerves and general state of health which can only be corrected after they reassess their motives.

○ **PEAK NUMBER 5** usually introduces significant changes to people's emotional state. These are created through the emergence of spiritual growth and understanding, which leads to greater personal freedom. It is a period through which the psychic powers undergo considerable strengthening, thereby facilitating an improved level of emotional control. In turn this lessens reactive behaviour to people and situations. As a consequence a greater measure of personal liberty develops that prepares the way for increased spiritual awareness. Those who in earlier years were anxious about their financial security now have the means to dispel such worry with a more balanced view of their real needs and environmental influences.

○ **PEAK NUMBER 6** brings with it a very strong power for creative development. It is a period when the highest spiritual and mental faculties can combine to reveal to us our vital role in the limitless plan of creation. Such sublime awareness will rarely become apparent to any but the more mature, more highly evolved people. For the majority, those who identify with physical possessiveness, this becomes a period of intense home involvement or, if unmarried, a hankering to settle down in their own home. Tendencies to worry about the home or to rush into marriage should be recognised as merely the procreative counterparts of what would otherwise be a powerful creative drive. Wisdom and patience should be exercised to avoid the need for the hurtful lessons that are attracted when emotions dominate people's affairs.

○ **PEAK NUMBER 7** can bring many surprising changes into people's lives. It is the period when we are called upon to share all we have learned so far. By so doing we experience tremendous progress in our own unfolding, for there is no better system of learning than that of teaching. This is an intensely empirical period in life, for it requires us to undergo much testing. If successful we qualify for the higher teachings that await us during this year; if we have not yet matured to a point of acceptable growth, we must spend more time in preparatory development. Most people during this period of vibrational influence are called upon to undertake some form of teaching, but not necessarily in conventional scholastic fields. More often their teaching is associated with post-academic fields of human evolvement such as yoga, natural therapies, spiritual awareness and artistic development.

○ **PEAK NUMBER 8** denotes independence as the prevailing force during this very powerful period. Whether independence develops through artistic or commercial involvements will, of course, depend on the Ruling Number: if it is an even number, financial success if indicated; if an odd number, success through artistic (or for some people academic) expression is more likely. Great care must be taken to use the power of this vibration constructively, and not let opposing individuals or limiting situations inhibit its transmission. The result of such influences will be clearly discernible in an uncharacteristic aloofness – the effort of the soul struggling to achieve independent expression.

○ **PEAK NUMBER 9** introduces a period of pronounced humanitarian activity. This vibration brings with it special opportunities to serve humankind. It is also a period when intense mental involvement is necessary for the greatest success to be achieved:

analysing and assessing the needs of others, planning for major changes in vocation and re-evaluating long-standing relationships and environmental surroundings. Many people attempt to make demands on your time and energy during this period. Some are in genuine need and provide important opportunities to serve; some will be artificially contrived to attract your sympathy. These latter cases should be treated as individuals needing awakening. Our discriminatory and analysing abilities will certainly be tested and strengthened by such experiences. While some people under this vibration will need to remain at home and be of service, others will be moved to travel to undergo important lessons in development.

Everyone, during the first year of influence following the attainment of this Peak, will find important changes occurring in their lives. If not involving travel, they will almost without exception move house, change jobs or form new circles of acquaintances. Any one of a number of these alterations in lifestyle can occur, depending on the nature of the responsibilities necessary to the prevailing stage in growth toward maturity.

○ **PEAK NUMBER** 10 can only occur on the third or fourth Pyramid Peaks, as maturity approaches its zenith. It brings a special strength, a unique power for relating to the needs of others during important periods of adjustment in their lives. This ability is the happy consequence of people's own living experiences and the training instilled by them. With the emphasis on mind power, as indicated by the 9 in every birth date last century, a considerable amount of mental adjustment is needed to remould outlooks and lifestyles as the New Age approaches. Older souls who have a Peak Number 10 during this period assume critically important roles in guiding and encouraging those in need. This is an exciting responsibility that confers upon the giver as many benefits as upon the receiver.

PEAK NUMBER 11 is the second of the two Peak Numbers that can occur on either the third or fourth Peaks. As with the Peak Number 10, a high level of maturity is necessary to handle its power. Peak Number 11 indicates that a considerable amount of spiritual accountability is demanded. Yet the demand will never exceed the individual's capacity. It is a period of high intuitiveness, when the most inspired actions become possible. However, there are certain spiritual requirements necessary for the optimum potential of this period to be realised. These involve compassion, temperance, integrity and the practice of meditation. Compassion means far more than its modern limited interpretation of commiseration and comfort. It is the practice of philanthropy, the sharing of love in its highest spiritual sense. In very practical terms it implies thoughtfulness for, and harmony with, all life, especially human life. Temperance is the expression of balance and moderation in all undertakings, while meditation is an exercise in enlightenment through a relaxed mind and body, restoring complete harmony. The virtue of impeccable integrity must prevail throughout actions and thoughts, thereby ensuring that no negative forces can impede spiritual blossoming, the supreme purpose of this period.

CHAPTER .12

The astrology numerology connection

This book is not designed to teach astrology; but astrological influences play such a powerful role in understanding personality and individuality that it would be impossible to omit the most salient features from our thorough discovery of the inner self. These features are primarily represented by the sun signs, for they are the dominant aspect of the numerological profile. This confers the essential link in the astrology numerology connection.

The close relationship between astrology and numerology is evident to all who have studied both. They both provide an insight into life, yet we always find an explicit preference with students and counsellors for one over the other. The basis for such preference will not always be apparent, nor does the reason really matter – an academic scientist might exert a similar preference for the study of physics over chemistry, yet they are so related that no worthy scientist can afford to be without a sound working knowledge of both.

This analogy between the two metaphysical sciences and the two physical sciences is appropriately illustrative, for it offers many parallels to our discoveries. Numerology and astrology are the two most scientific and reliable metaphysical sciences for the investigation into human personality and the discovery of our individuality. Physics and chemistry are two of the most essential physical sciences that involve the study of the material universe, the understanding of the outer self, the "doing" aspects of life. It is impossible to thoroughly understand human health without physics and chemistry, just as it is impossible to thoroughly understand the purpose of human life and how it can be best lived without numerology and the support of sun sign astrology.

To the sceptic, this will appear an extravagant claim, but the proof is in the practice. However, we need to acknowledge that many people are already prejudiced against astrology and as such should not let this aspect of my book detract from their interest in numerology. They can skip this chapter if they wish – or they can read on. If they choose to read on, they might acquire a little knowledge that may put their prejudices to question.

As one of the metaphysical keystones, astrology is more than the mere study of heavenly bodies. It is the ancient science of the study of the celestial bodies and their relationship to human life. Its origin far predates recorded history, lying possibly beyond the remote Atlantean period. We know that the people of Atlantis used it extensively, conferring their knowledge upon their fellow humankind on both sides of the ocean that was named after them. Yet, their influence was so profound that it permeated far beyond the shores of the Atlantic Ocean, with traces of it being extant in Central and South America, as well as in the western Mediterranean arc.

The ancients were not scientific people, as we understand the meaning of the word today. But they did recognise the powerful influence over their affairs exerted by the sun and the moon, along with the mysterious magnetism of the planets and the constellations. Not only were these influences apparent in the formation of the weather and the tides, but also in farming and, most appropriately, in human personality. Hence, these early studies evolved, revealing the influences exerted by various celestial bodies at the time of a person's birth.

With the establishment of the modern scientific system by Pythagoras, those ancient observations (for even then they were ancient) were expanded. Thereby the metaphysical sciences of numerology and astrology gained credibility.

There have always been people who have exploited the gullible. It is possibly even worse today than in ancient times. But it was the people who exploited numerology and astrology in ancient times, particularly those who used them as tools of divination during the biblical era, who gave them a spurious reputation. But that was long ago and bears no relationship to numerology and astrology as we know them today, any more than ancient blood-letting bears any relationship to modern medicine.

Clearly we must realise that numerology and astrology are not predictive arts to be used to hold the fear of a calamitous future over those they seek to exploit, as did the astrologers of Nebuchadnezzar's court whom Daniel exposed. They are valid metaphysical sciences by which the discovery of the inner self becomes the most attainable.

When a person is born, we know that certain vibrational influences prevail that can be analysed numerologically to reliably assess the individuality of that person. The basis of this assessment is, of course, the date of birth. Let us also realise that, at the time of such birth, the earth itself was receiving unique vibratory emanations from the sun and the sun's position in relation to other celestial bodies and constellations. This is the basis of astrology.

There are twelve astrological sun signs, each exerting an influence that lasts for a period averaging one calendar month. The twelve collectively total one full calendar year, one complete revolution of Earth around its sun. Today, astrology is so widely used (whether we like to admit it or not), that every person knows the name of their sun sign whether or not they understand what it represents in their life.

The following information is presented as representative of the salient features of each of the sun signs and their related factors. They are not intended to be exhaustive, for this would require a huge book in itself. Rather it is of maximum benefit to students of numerology to understand these essential features, with a special emphasis on the unique health aspects of the sun signs that will provide vital supplementary information for the purpose of achieving a desirable overall balance in life.

Usually, the zodiac is represented in circular form, but for our purposes, it is best illustrated in the rectangular chart form that you'll find on the following page. In this form, it clearly reveals relationships existing between the Triplicities and the elements, and between the Triplicities and the three Planes of expression as represented on the numerological Birth Chart.

TRIPLICITY (Lesson)	FIRE (Compassion)	EARTH (Service)	AIR (Brotherhood)	WATER (Peace)
HEAD Intellect Thought	ARIES Mar 21-Apr 20 Dynamic	TAURUS Apr 21-May 20 Steady	GEMINI May 21-Jun 20 Sensitive	CANCER Jun 21-Jul 21 Protective
MIDDLE Emotions Feeling	LEO Jul 22-Aug 22 Leadership	VIRGO Aug 23-Sep 22 Perfectionist	LIBRA Sep 23-Oct 22 Balance	SCORPIO Oct 23-Nov 22 Sex & Healing
FEET Understanding Doing	SAGITARIUS Nov 23-Dec 22 Gregarious	CAPRICORN Dec 23-Jan 21 Cautious	AQUARIUS Jan 22-Feb 20 Knowledge	PISCES Feb 21-Mar 20 Peacemakers

○ TRIPLICITIES

These are three major aspects of human expression that effectively divide the twelve sun signs into groups of four each. These three groups are closely related to the three groups of numbers on each of the three Planes of the Birth Chart. The first four signs, Aries, Taurus, Gemini and Cancer, belong to the Head Triplicity because of their strong emphasis on mental expression; just as the numbers 3, 6 and 9 belong to the Mind Plane of the Birth Chart due to their primary emphasis on mental expression. The second group of four signs, Leo, Virgo, Libra and Scorpio, belong to the Middle Triplicity in consequence of their dominant feeling nature and their strong emphasis on emotional expression; just as the numbers 2, 5 and 8 belong to the Soul Plane of the Birth Chart. The third group of four signs, Sagittarius, Capricorn, Aquarius and Pisces, comprise the Feet Triplicity because of their dominantly practical nature, seeking to understand the underlying purpose and origin of things; just as the numbers 1, 4 and 7 belong to the Practical Plane of the Birth Chart.

○ THE ELEMENTS

The ancients observed long before the recorded history of humankind that there are four basic aspects to human nature. To each of these, they symbolically related one of the essential physical elements of planet Earth: fire, earth, air and water. Observations by the ancient teachers recognised that each of the twelve sun signs manifested a basic characteristic relating to one of these four elements, yet each was expressed in a different way. Further observations related each of these elements to one of the four basic karmic lessons intended to be expressed by the human life involved.

○ **FIRE SIGNS** of Aries, Leo and Sagittarius are typified by fast-moving, volatile, passionate people with abundant nervous energy. Their major lesson in life is to understand the meaning of divine love, embracing compassion and philanthropy by attuning to the needs of others and by providing loving support for the attainment of those needs. This will assist people with a fire sign to become less impetuous and to attain more method and order in their affairs.

○ **EARTH SIGNS** of Taurus, Virgo and Capricorn reveal steady rather predictable people who are the most consistent and dependable friends we are likely to find. Their primary karmic lesson involves being of service to other people, by which means they will elevate their own consciousness beyond the physical to the spiritual (but this is rarely achieved before the latter half of their years of maturity). Primary motivations in their earlier years are more related to the physical world of playing, eating and doing, for it is through these involvements that they acquire the early development they need.

○ **AIR SIGNS** of Gemini, Libra and Aquarius are the flexible people with quick, mercurial brains, yet with a deep understanding of life and people. They possess tremendous mental versatility and are able to think of many diverse things at the same time, but this can lead to fragmentation and a serious depletion of nervous energy (enervation). Through their karmic lesson of sisterhood, they learn to be of help to others, by which means they develop a deep philosophy of life.

○ **WATER SIGNS** of Cancer, Scorpio and Pisces are the signs of the more peaceful people – peaceful most of the time. In their natural composure, they are quiet, restful beings whose presence usually brings comfort. Yet at times, these people can be very emotional and can lose control of their feelings, which they must guard against or they create distress to all involved and noticeably diffuse their natural peacefulness. They have great tenacity and are exceptionally capable healers when living constructively.

○ THE CUSPS

The influence of each of the twelve sun signs lasts approximately one month of each year, with the commencing and concluding days falling on or close to the dates shown on the chart. But the change over from one sun sign to the next does not occur with the suddenness of turning a tap on and off. Rather, there is a brief transition period of some six days, three either side of the nominal date. This period is known as the cusp, during which the influences of both signs prevail, one diminishing, the other intensifying. The relationship between the joint influences of each sign is generally indicated by the precise position of the birth date within the cusp. For instance the cusp of Aries-Taurus covers the inclusive period of April 18 to 23. From April 18, the influence of Aries diminishes, yet is still stronger than the rising influence of Taurus. This will be so until after April 20 (on which date both signs exert influences of somewhat equal strength), when the rising influence of Taurus will be stronger. By April 24, Aries will exert no influence – it will be totally that of Taurus.

The cusp consideration is somewhat analogous to that of the transition between the personal growth cycle years as revealed in Chapter 9. But the concept of cusps does not occur with Ruling Numbers, the numerological equivalent of astrology's sun signs. Ruling Numbers are precise for each birth date, changing abruptly at midnight to the consecutive number. And consecutive Ruling Numbers, as revealed in Chapter 7, are clearing different to each other.

○ FOOD AND HEALTH

All too frequently, books on metaphysics overlook the importance of the three-fold integration of body-mind-soul. I hope to offer my readers the bonus of discovering more about their health than is usually offered in such a book. Now that we are dealing with some of the more specific aspects of health as revealed through the astrological sun signs, particular foods will be recommended as indicated by each sun sign. Of course, one can also take the recommended homoeopathic cell salts as well to hasten recovery from any recognised deficiencies; but the cell salts without the foods will be far less effective.

It is important to note that when taking the cell salts, do so in tablet form at least fifteen minutes before each meal, holding the tablets under the tongue until they dissolve. Generally, three tablets are taken at a time, though this depends on their potency – your practitioner should be able to guide you correctly.

Due to their high level of nutritional potency, some of the foods appear in the lists of more than one sign. You cannot improve upon unsalted nuts, raw seeds, soya beans, green vegetables and sprouts, together with many of the dried fruits and grains, as natural sources of almost the entire range of nutrients, especially the biochemic cell salts, required by the human body for optimum health. Some people are allergic to some foods; avoid those foods and substitute others if you know of your allergies. If you have been tested, see your practitioner and arrange for a food tolerance test. Some people cannot digest raw nuts as well as they can dry roasted nuts – do what's best for you. Nowhere are recommendations made for the use of dairy products (especially cow's milk), common salt or fast foods – rarely are any of these conducive to good health.

○ ARIES – MARCH 21 TO APRIL 20

Characteristic expression

Arians have very active brains, always seeking to learn things, always thinking and planning. They are high-spirited people, dynamic, volatile, courageous, witty and potentially very good scholars. Learning is important to them, as are bright social associations. They are rarely lost for words and ever ready to verbally defend themselves and their actions. For those who live constructively, responsibility is their second nature; in its expression they find their acute intuition gives them constant guidance. The other side of their nature is to be reckless, headstrong and often quite fierce – this is when they live destructively and become a liability to society. Factors that could swing the personality away from its naturally constructive expression are often traced to mineral deficiency in the diet, particularly of the most vital cell salt for Arians, potassium phosphate.

Negative tendencies to be surmounted

Due to the high level of cerebral energy, Arians can be extremely impatient with others. However, with a loved one they can show so much patience as to be easily imposed upon. This will effectively reduce the reliability of their intuition and cause them to make some monumental errors of judgement. Even when living constructively they should take care not to overestimate their capabilities or to engage in repeatedly lengthy periods of mental activity without balancing such periods with relaxation; such neglect will lead to enervation, headaches and recklessness. They must think before speaking, especially if they intend to be critical, for Arians have a sharp tongue and a fiery temper when they lose self-control.

Health aspects

Aries relates to the cerebrum, the human brain. Hence a physical characteristic usually related to Arians is a large head. They often have a larger than average brain and require a diet that will provide extra nourishment to the brain cells and nerve fluid. The bio-chemic cell salt most useful in this regard is known as Kali Phos – potassium phosphate. It can be consumed in a supplementary form as a powder or liquid. But if while taking this supplement the Arian adheres to a conventional, high acid diet based on processed and refined foods, a high meat intake, tea, coffee and or alcohol, their hyperacid condition will negate the alkalising benefits of the cell salts. They are far better advised to alter their diet to include natural foods, with special emphasis on those richest in natural potassium phosphate, as listed (according to availability):

- Yeast – edible brewer's and torula varieties
- Soya grits and, for those who want milk, soya or rice milk
- Soya beans – soaked for twenty four hours then steamed
- Wheatgerm and wheat bran – both must be fresh and raw
- Sunflower seeds – either sprouted or as raw whole kernels
- Chickpeas (garbanzos) and lentils
- Raw, unsalted nuts – especially almonds, brazils and pistachios
- Rye – sprouted is best, next is freshly stoneground

A deficiency of potassium phosphate can be generally recog-nised as affecting mental processes manifesting in such symptoms as migraine, extreme nervousness, frequent hysteria, mental exhaustion, psychosis, paranoia, wild fancies and forebodings, and so on.

Karmic lesson

Arians must learn the meaning of selfless love, recognising its marked difference to physical desire. Compassion is the highest expression of universal love, so this virtue must become a part of their every thought, word and deed. Vital to the development of compassion is the mastery of emotions, especially temper, anger and jealousy.

○ TAURUS – APRIL 21 TO MAY 20

Characteristic expression

Taureans are dominating, strong and persistent people who find their easiest form of expression through movement. They are extremely stable and solid friends, highly reliable and predictable. They are also very orthodox, which makes them slow to accept new ideas. Taurus governs the cerebellum, the lower brain and the nerve centre regulating physical movement; hence the initial response from a Taurean to do something rather than think about it. This creates reactions rather than actions, giving rise to emotional involvement and passionate expression. Nevertheless, this is an Earth sign, a stabilising influence that balances the emotions unless some extreme irritation persists. In the normal course of events these people have kindly dispositions and are slow to anger. But when ultimately aroused, they become volcanic. Once they explode is it as though they have blown off excess steam from their escape valve, which in turn allows them to return to an equilibrium. A further influence of earth is observed in the Taurean love for comfort, financial security and the good things in life – especially rich food. They have to learn that rich food is rarely a good choice for the body.

Negative tendencies to be surmounted

Impulsive desire plays too great a part in the life of Taureans. They must learn to reason more and to think carefully before doing – then they will act rather than react. Their constancy should never be allowed to become obstinacy; their generosity should not prompt them to become over-indulgent. Obstinacy and over-indulgence are emotional reactions that are often resorted to when fear prevails: fear of change, fear of being disliked or fear of being insecure. The cerebellum is often referred to as the animal brain, for it dominates the unconscious, the body's movement and its passions. Special care should be taken to avoid emotional excess, for passion cannot hear the voice of reason.

Health aspects

Taurus exerts strong influence on the ears, neck, throat, liver and gall bladder. People born under this sign may have large ears, a strong neck and powerful voice (many become successful wrestlers or singers). It is not uncommon for Taureans to have weight problems brought about primarily by their tendency to overindulge in rich food and to retain excess water in the body. The biochemic cell salt, Nat Sulph – sodium sulphate – is aligned with Taurus, because this is the most efficient expeller of water. Deficiency in this salt will induce pains in the back of the neck, which sometimes run down the spine affecting the liver. As this cell salt is vital to the body's elimination of water, its lack will cause the body to resort to the next best means: it will produce nerve and muscular spasms, thereby inducing feverishness from the violent effort to throw off excess moisture via the bloodstream through perspiration. This also effectively reduces the body's toxicity level. The alternate fever and chill as the body cleanses then normalises itself, together with the muscular aches from the spasms, give rise to the disease that continues to baffle physicians who have given it the name influenza. Taureans in hot and humid climates, where the air is supercharged with moisture and people drink more (which, in turn, impedes their digestion and nutrient absorption), run greater risk of moisture retention. This often produces biliousness and sometimes predisposes toward malaria. The habit of adding common salt (sodium chloride) to foods must be avoided as this chemical works against the body's efforts to eliminate excess moisture. Contrary to popular opinion, common salt does not avert dehydration or cramps; it is a mild poison, which is the reason the body works to throw it off through its pores. A diet comprised of foods rich in natural sodium sulphate, will also be found to contain adequate natural sodium chloride to facilitate proper cellular chemical balance. The diet should also be low in saturated fatty acids and cholesterol to ease the strain on the liver, gall bladder and arteries. Some of the most desirable foods include abundant fresh salad vegetables, particularly sprouts, celery and carrots. Dried fruits such as figs, raisins and sultanas are also exceptionally nourishing to Taureans. One meal a day of fresh fruits, eaten raw, is definitely beneficial, particularly as the first meal of the day.

Karmic lesson

To recognise the difference between the imprudent emotional reactions and balanced rational actions provides one of the most vital experiences in the life of a person born under the sign of Taurus. It is through service to humankind that they will learn to acquire mastery over their desires and emotions. Consequently, they will always be led into activities that will allow them such experiences.

○ GEMINI – MAY 21 TO JUNE 20

Characteristic expression

Here we are obliged to consider two people in one. Symbolically represented as the twins, the sign of Gemini indicates two personalities: one relates to the innate individuality, the other relates to the personality of social intercourse. Belonging to the Air sign of the Head Triplicity, Gemini people are extremely sensitive and subject to rapid change of thought without warning. Their fast-moving brains tend to give them a mercurial nature, but this also implies some very beneficial abilities; viz. a reliable sense of discrimination and a gift of communication. To be instantly able to discriminate between sense and nonsense, truth and falsehood, reality and unreality, is characteristic of Geminis. So, too, is their ability to communicate their ideas in writing; they convey their thoughts more freely this way than they can usually do verbally.

Negative tendencies to be surmounted

The twin personalities of the Gemini have the disadvantage of confusing people, and even Geminis themselves can be uncertain of how to react to different situations. In general, they tend to oscillate between their lower and higher selves, their emotional and spiritual natures. Once they learn not to react, but to thoughtfully consider first, they will not be so drawn to the emotional. Until then they will find their power of concentration diminishing, with a corresponding increase in uncertainty and nervousness. Rest and relaxation are prime requisites that help to keep their nerves under control. They should become involved in the arts, including singing, playing an instrument, painting, pottery making, and so on. This will provide balance to their lives and is an excellent balm for their nervous system.

Health aspects

Usually the most noticeable features of Gemini bodies are their strong shoulders, arms and hands. Their major weakness lies in their respiratory passages, with congestion a common problem. The most important of the twelve biochemic cell salts for the Gemini is Kali Mur – potassium chloride. This is both an essential blood nourisher and a vital nutrient for the proper formation of fibrin, the elastic fibrous protein that regulations the formation of the skin and hair. A deficiency of potassium chloride can cause a thickening of fibrin, menstrual irregularities, and or congestion when located in the respiratory passages. This might manifest as pleurisy, catarrh, pneumonia, diphtheria or bronchitis. If the congested fibrin is not thrown out of the bloodstream it can create embolisms that might clog the auricles and ventricles of the heart, ultimately causing it to stop. The most satisfactory manner by which to obtain adequate potassium chloride is through the diet. Foods richest in natural potassium chloride are listed below, according to its concentration:

- Kelp – powder and granules
- Yeast – brewer's and torula
- Avocados
- Coconut meat – fresh
- Dried fruits
- Most fresh vegetables, especially sprouts, asparagus, cabbage, carrot, celery, eggplant, kohlrabi, lettuce, parsnip and tomato

Karmic lesson

All people born under the Air signs are motivated by a yearning for sisterhood, yet this is less obvious in the expression of the Gemini than in the Libran or Aquarian. The strong mentality of the Gemini, especially evident in their analytical approach to life and to people, is inclined to make them appear more egocentric than they are in reality. This is further aggravated by a difficulty in verbal expression, which is so often a part of the Gemini nature. Deep within, Geminis know that they often misrepresent themselves. Though this is not intentional, they do not know how to correct it. They will find release from this quandary when they acknowledge the yearning in the depths of their souls for love, companionship and understanding – in a word, sisterhood. As Geminis mature, they become more aware of the importance of compassion and their relationships with other people.

○ CANCER – JUNE 21 TO JULY 21

Characteristic expression

The astrological term Cancer derives from the Latin for crab and has no relationship to the malignant disease. The disease was so-called because of its tumorous nature and unrestrained reproductive ability. Symbolically, the crab tells us much about the motivation and expression of people born under this sign. They are persistent, cautious and prudent, with a deeply sensitive and tender nature. Their perseverance is enforced by a cultivated hardness, an acquired protection of sensitive feelings. They are home loving, with a deep concern for their castle and the wellbeing of all within it. Their love for children is often satisfied by producing large families, for which their robust reproductive organs stand them in good stead. A further crab-like expression is the fondness these people have of collecting things for which they have no immediate use or prospect of use. Especially pronounced is the protectiveness and tenacity of those born under the sign of Cancer. These traits underlie so much of their endeavour – physical, emotional and mental. They possess a naturally good memory and strive to retain this important attribute (memory being tenacity of thought). Cancerians are often drawn to health-related fields, for they are natural healers with a deep concern for human welfare.

Negative tendencies to be surmounted

The acute sensitivity of Cancerians must be recognised as vital to their spiritual growth and to their loving concern for others. But unless they have achieved a reasonable level of mastery, these people risk the decline of their strengths by becoming victims of their own emotions. These are manifested as nervous outbursts and moodiness, creating considerable drains on their energy reserves. Parents must be especially careful to train their Cancerian children to gain confidence in themselves and their feelings and not to react emotionally to apparent thoughtfulness demonstrated by less sensitive people. Unless they are carefully trained in self-discipline, these children could become reclusive and very shy, especially if they have the Arrow of Hypersensitivity. In practice, I have found many people who believe they are suffering from hypoglycemia are, in reality, suffering acute enervation induced by lack of control of their extreme sensitivity and worry. This applies particularly to people born under the sign of Cancer. They are inclined to worry about things of a domestic nature, especially the home and the welfare of their children when away from home. Fear of financial insecurity is also a great source of worry for many Cancerians. Unless these anxieties and torments are controlled, mental imbalance could follow.

Health aspects

The sign of Cancer exerts its major influence in the chest, spleen, solar plexus and stomach. People with this sun sign must be very careful with their diet because they do not have strong stomachs and easily succumb to gastric problems. When associated with worry this gives a fine prescription for ulcers. Simple, natural foods should comprise their basic diet because Cancerians must assiduously avoid highly seasoned or highly preserved foods, such as curry, peppers, pickles, strong cheeses, heavily-spiced continental-type foods, and so on. The most vital biochemic cell salt for Cancerians is calcium fluoride, the cell salt that plays an essential role in the development and maintenance of the brain membranes, as well as the eyes, teeth, bones and internal cellular structure of the skin. A deficiency of this mineral salt will result from a diet lacking in green vegetables, sprouts, carrots, unsalted raw nuts or mild cheeses (especially cottage). These foods are excellent sources of natural calcium fluoride. Such deficiencies can result in cracked skin (loss of cellular elasticity), especially between the toes or fingers, around the anus or the mouth; early loss of memory and or the development of an anxiety complex; cataracts in the eyes; and, for women, very painful periods and, ultimately, weakened reproductive organs.

Karmic lesson

By using the mind to attain a degree of emotional control, and by conserving nervous energy, we achieve the most precious of all possessions – inner peace. Such is the essential lesson to be pursued by Cancerians. Self-control is not always easily achieved, but then, neither is anything of lasting value attained without effort. As soon as they learn to channel their sensitivities into avenues of healing and human welfare, Cancerians will have made significant progress in acquiring this harmonising peace.

○ LEO – JULY 22 TO AUGUST 22

Characteristic expression

Leos are natural leaders and as alert (sometimes as aggressive) as the lion by which they are symbolised. They have considerable confidence in their own abilities and are unhappy working under authority. They are affectionate and possess enormous reserves of energy, which gives them exceptional drive and intrepid expression. Leos can also be of two extremely different natures: creative or destructive. A lot of them are emotional, reactive, desire-motivated people, with a reputation for instability and volatility. The more enlightened Leos are as yet in the minority, though growing aware-ness among New Age people is swinging the pendulum. When they discover the secrets of self-control, Leo people are able to exercise their extremely powerful will for the common good and to express themselves creatively as enlightened examples of divine power in human action. They have a naturally deep sympathy for the less fortunate or those in trouble – not unexpected from peo-ple with such acute sensitivity.

Negative tendencies to be surmounted

Care must always be exercised in the handling of powerful sources of energy, particularly fiery human energy. With their exceptional drive, Leos are inclined to overtax their heart and nerves unless they learn to practise meditation or, at the least, to incorporate periods of relaxation into their daily routines. They must expressly avoid arguments and disruptive emotional involvements such as sordid love affairs and similar philandering, for these will heavily tax their emotions, considerably depleting nervous energy. While they avidly enjoy emotional expression, Leo people must exercise moderation to ensure they do not lose control of their feelings.

They are inclined to anger easily, but this will only further deplete their nervous energy. Anger places enormous strain on the muscles of the heart, far more than most people realise. Care must be taken that their natural sympathy is not imposed upon by thoughtless people, for if their sympathy is exploited it can cause such sensitive people to feel very let down, even bitter.

Health aspects

The heart, motor nerves (which regulate movement) and the blood are intimately related and are the most vulnerable components of the Leo body. Thus, they must ensure that their diet is regulated to avoid too many acid-forming foods or substances such as tea, coffee, excessive protein-rich foods, chocolate, sweets, alcohol, white flour products, and so on. In view of their emotional tendencies, which strain the nerves and the heart, it is not surprising that Leos often suffer from a deficiency of the mineral cell salt Mag Phos – magnesium phosphate. This is the important nutrient involved in regulating nerve and muscle impulses, especially those that govern the function of the heart. There is a tendency for anyone suffering from a lack of magnesium phosphate to experience spells of crying, laughter, coughing, sneezing, hiccoughs or cramps, or to become quite reckless in manner. These symptoms are highly enervating but will be greatly relieved by the therapeutic application of a few grams of Mag Phos in a glass of hot water. Many sufferers from angina pectoris and mild heart spasms can overcome these acute disorders by attaining better control of their emotions and by including in their diet foods known to be natural sources of magnesium phosphate, particularly the following (listed in order of richness):

Σ

- Wheatgerm and bran
- Raw, unsalted nuts and seeds
- Yeast – brewer's and torula
- Soya beans, soya milk and soya grits
- Wholewheat and rye – as cereals or in wholegrain bread
- Rolled oats
- Millet and buckwheat
- Brown lentils – especially nourishing when sprouted and eaten raw
- Blackstrap molasses

Karmic lesson

Every person born under the sign of Leo is aware of their strong inner drive. Those who have not learned to channel this tremendous energy are often impatient and difficult to live with due to their frequent emotional eruptions. Life is the tamer of the lion, taking the wild animal nature and gently transforming it until it becomes a moderated, harnessed force, willing and able to be directed by the supreme intelligence. Then will the lion allow divine order to be established in all its affairs. Deep within, they are warm and compassionate people, but many Leos are not ready to exhibit this beautiful side of their nature until they reach the third phase of life (fulfilment). Life will be much more rewarding for them and for those with whom they associate when they learn to be more compassionate in their earlier years. This is the Leo's major lesson in life.

◦ VIRGO – AUGUST 23 to SEPTEMBER 22

Characteristic expression

The symbol of Virgo is the virgin, meaning pure, perfect and impeccable. This accurately relates to both the nature and the body of those whose sun sign is Virgo. They are perfectionists, with an all-consuming concern in matters of health, yet with bodies that often experience elimination problems. In their search for perfection, Virgo people are discriminatory and analytical, demanding accuracy and detail. They never cease striving for these qualities. Virgos make firm friends, often seeking to help others improve their own lives. At times this makes them appear critical, but rarely is there anything of a condemnatory nature in their criticisms. As a rule they are more critical of themselves than of others, for they recognise that perfection must develop from within. Virgos have a natural ability for healing, but must guard against becoming over-anxious about their own health. Such anxiety can give rise to hypochondriacal tendency, with its resultant morbidity and mild depression. This negates the natural healing ability of their bodies, defeating their aim to improve the quality of life for all.

Negative tendencies to be surmounted

This tendency towards overanxiety is very prevalent with Virgo people, yet they rarely have any real cause for worry. A similar response is also found in their work lives where, if compelled to accept considerable responsibility, they become apprehensive of their ability. This has the effect of undermining their self-confidence. Virgos work best under encouraging, appreciative direction – and they actively seek to become involved in work. But their striving for perfection can become quite obsessive, that is until they sensibly relate it to practicalities. Virgos must guard against becoming emotional as a result of frustration, for indeed they will experience much frustration until moderation is learned. Some younger souls will be tempted to seek gratification through the sexual organs, excusing this desire for sensation as their right to love. Such justification might temporarily satisfy their egos, but their real motives never escape the Akashic Records, that total karmic history of experiences transmitted through the High Self.

Health aspects

Some schools of astrology relate the procreative organs to Virgo but this can be misleading. Such a relationship only exists when Virgos live negatively and seek to escape the frustration that arises from the experiences intended to be their lessons. When living positively, Virgos actually place less emphasis on the sexual side of life than do many other people. The organs of the body most influenced by this sign are the solar plexus nerve region and the organs of elimination (bowels, pores and nasal passages). The bowels and skin play a vital role in the health of every person but they are especially important for the Virgo. There is a tendency for them to suffer from clogged pores, creating a dry skin and impeding the elimination of toxic matter through perspiration. The skin's seven million pores also regulate the body's temperature. This function, too, will be inhibited when the pores are clogged by a thickening of the skin's tissue oil. This obstruction is caused by a deficiency in the mineral salt Kali Sulph – potassium sulphate. Those toxic wastes that the body cannot adequately eliminate by perspiring remain in the body and must then be processed by the respiratory tract or the bowels. The blocking of the pores also tends to raise the body's temperature, forcing it to work harder to reprocess the waste matter. This double action further increases the body's temperature, producing what we call colds, accompanied by sluggish bowels.

Sometimes this creates the feeling of suffocation, with hot flushes and a craving for cold air. Other symptoms of impaired elimination are catarrhal and asthmatic congestion, severe nerve pains in the region of the solar plexus (particularly painful to Virgo women during menopause), dandruff, baldness, skin eruptions and conjunctivitis. Foods in which potassium sulphate occurs naturally will greatly assist the body's cleansing efforts. Those richest in the cell salt are:

- Green vegetables – especially brussels sprouts and watercress
- Deep sea kelp – powder and granules
- Raw hazelnuts, Brazil nuts and chestnuts
- Dried figs and raisins
- Avocado, carrots, corn and eggplant

Karmic lesson

Being an Earth sign, Virgo indicates the need for useful service to humankind, making it necessary for those born under its influence to acquire critical karmic lessons. Suitably achieved through the practice of healing or the arts, it must always be selfless service. They must learn that awareness cannot be achieved when undue emphasis is directed towards the physical body or its lusting for sensational involvements. Freedom, we must remember, is only achieved to the extent that the mind is free from ignorance and the emotions do not cloud sensitivity.

o LIBRA – SEPTEMBER 23 TO OCTOBER 22

Characteristic expression

Balance is the most noteworthy endowment of people born under this sign, which is symbolised by the scales. The natural inclination of Librans is gentleness, for they are very affectionate individuals with an intense desire to live in peace and harmony, and to create such an atmosphere wherever they go. They become utterly disenchanted above all with dishonest people in public office, finding it impossible to excuse any form of hypocrisy, meanness or shallowness. Librans see marvellous perfection in nature – not the perfection of mathematical symmetry, but the beautiful symphony of the great struggle between the material universe and nature working inexorably towards order. They especially abhor bloodshed and violence of any type, for such transgression threatens balance and offends beauty. Librans are blessed with a highly perceptive insight and a keen sense of justice, a combination that predisposes them to expressions of frankness often more forthright than flattering. It must be realised that they intend no personal malice by their directness but, rather, seek to correct anything they consider undesirable or outside the appropriate order of things.

Negative tendencies to be surmounted

It will be surprising for many people who know Librans to learn that they are naturally peaceful, gentle and affectionate beings. Often negative Librans express themselves in emotional tempestuousness, recklessness and sometimes downright aggressiveness. They also succumb to sexual excesses when their health is unsettled. But it must be emphasised that this is not the natural portrait of a Libran, nor of any well-balanced person. A natural balance of expression is precariously dependent upon the body's chemical balance and when this becomes upset by acidic irritations, the brain, nerves and muscles are directly affected. Such internal disharmonies induce actions that are actually in conflict with the individual's real nature. They may be tense, excitable, aggressive or even suicidal in their confusion. Rarely are they aware that internal disharmony is a frequent cause of such attitudes. Therefore, they are not easily convinced that their diet has more influence over their emotions than the environmental factors they prefer to blame, such as the weather, the politicians, the spouse, and so on.

Health aspects

Hyperacidity, in these days of highly processed, non-nutritive foods, is far from uncommon. Most people live it, believing it to be their natural condition. Consequently, most people tend to be emotionally unstable, easily irritated and readily aggressive. But when this condition prevails for Librans, the departure from their normal and natural mode of expression becomes extreme and critically interferes with their basic purpose in life. One of the most alkalising of the mineral cell salts required by the body is Nat Phos – sodium phosphate. A vital role of this nutrient is to restore the body's chemical balance with its strong alkalinity. Not only must Librans ensure that their diet includes foods rich in this mineral salt, but they should also minimise (preferably avoid) highly processed, acid-forming foods of the modern diet such as white flour and white sugar products, canned foods, carbonated beverages, tea and coffee, and so on. Foods rich in natural sodium phosphate (in order of concentration):

○ Egg yolks
○ Raw salad vegetables – especially celery, sprouts, beetroot and carrots
○ Brewer's yeast
○ Dried fruits – especially figs, raisins and sultanas
○ Sunflower seed kernels – raw and sprouted

Fresh fruit is also an excellent alkalising food and a natural source of high energy fruit sugar (fructose). Each day would be a brighter one if it began with a fresh fruit salad. A daily vegetable salad is also indispensable to Librans, to help them to maintain a proper chemical balance. Without such a diet the body will manifest many of the following uncomfortable symptoms of hyperacidity: foul breath, pimples, skin irritations, frontal headaches (often with a feeling of intense cranial pressure), scabby ears that might emit a creamy discharge and feel constantly hot, ulcers, canker sores, rheumatism, diarrhoea and occasional convulsions (especially in children). Parents will also notice that children grind their teeth in sleep if their upper gastrointestinal tract is too acidic. This is often an indication of insufficient fresh fruit and vegetables in the diet. Bodily organs that are especially sensitive for Librans are the kidneys, bladder and adrenal glands – in fact, the entire pelvic region must be carefully looked after to avoid prolapsed organs. Keep the abdominal muscles in good tone through exercise. The lumbar region of the spine is also highly sensitive – lumbago and rheumatism are not uncommon for Librans.

Karmic lesson

People born under the sign of Libra are rarely content to pass through life without a marriage partner. For them the pairing of male with female is natural for personal balance and wholeness, as the marital partner serves to supply a counterbalance for the other's limitations. It is through such companionship, as well as through comradeship with others met as they travel through life, that Librans discover the meaning of sisterhood, sharing and expanding their awareness of life's purpose for themselves and all humankind. Sisterhood also teaches emotional control to those Librans who are motivated by the negative tendencies of jealousy, resentment and similarly unbalanced attitudes.

○ SCORPIO – OCTOBER 23 to NOVEMBER 22

Characteristic expression

As the last sign the Middle line of emotions and feeling, Scorpio relates to the most feeling, most sensitive parts of the body, viz. the reproductive organs. Hence, so much of the expression of those born under this sun sign has its motivation related to sex and secrecy. The men are more sexually oriented than the women of Scorpio, and are therefore much more emotional; the women are more able to contain their emotions and to direct their energies into healing and creativity. Both men and women have powerful determination and the ability to hide turbulent emotions beneath a façade of apparent calmness. Both are skilful with their hands, a special quality that, when related to their natural healing ability, explains why many are found in the field of health. Both the men and the women make excellent magnetic healers, chiropractors and osteopaths – those who prefer the more conventional aspects of the healing arts gravitate toward surgery and medicine. Their natural sensitivity gives these people reliable intuitive guidance when they are in command of their emotions. Their love of secrecy translates this power into successful professional conduct.

Negative tendencies to be surmounted

Being so impressionable and sensitive, Scorpios must guard against losing command of their feelings and becoming negatively emotional. Scorpio women are far more capable of controlling their emotions in early life. Than are the men of this sign Both can, however, achieve successful self-mastery during their years of maturity, though this often has to be forced upon them by necessary emotional lessons involving the heart. These demanding trials are required for the sole purpose of directing their steps further along the Path (towards perfection). During their period of emotional adolescence, some Scorpios can become so disturbed that for a time they appear quite bitter and cruel, unreliable and erratic. This is not their true nature, as is evident when personal maturity evolves from self-discipline. Men take longer to achieve this maturity than do women under the Scorpio influence – the reason why marriage between two Scorpios is rarely successful. A note of warning must be given here for Scorpio men: if too much emphasis is directed towards the careless abuse of sex, nervous energy can become seriously depleted. This will be particularly noticeable in the lower limbs, for the sciatic nerves are the most vulnerable. Resulting enervation can predispose towards painful physical constrictions, such as stiffness of the legs and thighs, curvature of the spine, paralysis, premature old age and senility.

Health aspects

We have already considered some pathological problems affecting Scorpio people as a consequence of their negative living. These are mostly related to the reproductive organs because they are the most sensitive organs in the Scorpio anatomy. Scorpio people have to learn that this region of the body is intended primarily for the begetting of children and for the spontaneous physical expression of overwhelming love between two people. It should not be regarded as a regular playground for overstimulated desires. The Kundalini, or divine creative force within humans, cannot be expressed creatively (upward) and for procreation (downward or sexually) at the same time. When too frequently involved in procreative expression, the Kundalini draws heavily upon the blood's vitality, resulting in a deficiency of the mineral biochemic salt important to Scorpios, Cal Sulph – calcium sulphate. Even if sexual expression is not actually practised, but is suppressed, almost as much bodily depletion will result. The natural alternative is creative expression, the elevation of Kundalini into practical service for the betterment of life. So absorbed are the enlightened Scorpios in their creativity that they must take care not to overdo their enthusiasm and drain their nervous energy in this direction by long hours of work with inadequate periods of relaxation. Symptoms of depleted calcium sulphate can be recognised in the body as burning sensations in the feet, anus, stomach, throat or mouth; sometimes as stomach ulcers, slow healing wounds, skin ailments and pimples. Loose bowels, not necessarily diarrhoea, can also be the result of insufficient dietary Cal Sulph. Further evidence of deficiency can be recognised in outward emotional agitation, even before it becomes a source of discomfort within the body. Foods offering important sources of natural calcium sulphate and which should be included in the regular diet of Scorpios are:

- Natural cheeses – especially Swiss and cheddar
- All green vegetables – especially watercress and parsley
- Molasses – but only for people who do not eat sufficient salads
- Raw, unsalted nuts – especially Brazil nuts
- Dried figs
- Raw, fresh egg yolks
- Sunflower seed kernels – raw and sprouted

Karmic lesson

It might seem incongruous that the sign of Scorpio is on the Middle line of emotions and feeling, yet is one of the Water Triplicity, which indicates the general lesson of peace. This indicates that of all the signs, those born under the influence of Scorpio have the most difficult lesson – the lesson of attaining peace through the mastery of the passions and the positive direction of kundalini energy. People are not only born under this sign when such a need has been karmically established, but also when their latent ability for healing has to be developed as a positive force in bringing bodily harmony to humankind.

○ SAGITTARIUS —
  NOVEMBER 23 TO DECEMBER 22

Characteristic Expression

Particularly characteristic of all healthy Sagittarians is their cheerful, gregarious manner. They are exceptionally good natured people who are always fond of company and involvement in physical activity. Yet they rarely allow people to get too close to them, preferring to maintain a safe distance to ensure their personal freedom. This independence is vital to them, and in turn they respect its need in other people's lives. Their delight in physical activity extends to many different sports but especially those that involve marked athletic ability. Sagittarians invariably possess very strong thighs and can usually move fast on their feet. This, coupled with their gregariousness, indicates why they are more interested in travel and constant movement than they are in static security or deep mental contemplation. When young they tend to shy away from too much responsibility but are prepared to accept their share as they mature. Sagittarians have a deep compassion for all living creatures. They also have a deep natural love of philosophy, which they should develop to better understand the purpose of life. Their responsiveness to laws, those of humanity and spirit, invariably results in their accepting both without question or objection. A noteworthy metaphysical quality possessed by most Sagittarians is their prophetic ability to foresee certain events. These sometimes manifest in dreams, but do not always involve them personally.

However, disbelief and discouragement when they are young invariably cause them to disregard this faculty. If nurtured, this ability could develop into a very powerful endowment, providing considerable benefit to many.

Negative tendencies to be surmounted

The desire for constant change can certainly lead into many and varied avenues of learning, but if allowed to persist unchecked it produces a taxing of mental faculties. Concentration and patience will be weakened unless self-control is adequately exercised. One of the most successful methods to achieve this is by emphasising accuracy in action. Accuracy is an excellent exercise in care, control and close mental application. Without the acknowledgment and practice of this, the Sagittarian can easily become motivated by idle desire and whim, experiencing much frustration and, ultimately, loneliness. Symptoms of deterioration will often appear as attitudes sharply alternating between faith and doubt, exhilaration and despondency. Eventually, nervous instability will become so intense as to create a highly neurotic person, unless they respond to self-discipline.

Health aspects

The human body comprises virtually every known element and it has combined them to form a countless number of chemical compounds. The chemicals that make up a building, the soil and the ocean are all similar to those within the human body, though in different proportions. Even the basic material of glass – sand – is not excluded, for it is this mineral, silicon oxide, that is one of the indispensable biochemic cell salts in the body. In fact, silicon oxide is the cell salt that is most important to the Sagittarians. Silica, as it is commonly known, is also quartz and is composed of extremely sharp crystals. In this regard, it symbolises the Sagittarian, the archer, with the sharp arrow that pierces its target. When silica is tempered to a high enough point for fusion it becomes crystal clear, as do the thoughts of the Sagittarian when their self-command and awareness have been tempered by the fusion of self-control with adequate experience. Silica is found in the skin and nails of the human body – it gives that natural glossy look to the hair. It is also present in the membrane covering that protects the bones and nerves. In general, this mineral is one of the most important strengtheners within the body. An insufficient supply is indicated by difficulty in thinking clearly, despondency, red eyelids, red nostrils with sore tips, acne and pimples on the face, boils, muffled hearing and catarrhal conditions of the upper respiratory tract. Natural foods found to be rich in silica are (in order of available quantity):

- All green vegetables – especially lettuce, parsley, asparagus and cucumber
- Fresh strawberries
- Sunflower seed kernels – raw and sprouted
- Raw pumpkin seed kernels (pepitas)
- Dried figs and sundried apricots

Karmic lesson

With their natural love of philosophy and their deep compassion for life, Sagittarians are well equipped to develop an excellent level of emotional control and mental stability. This will stand them in good stead for a highly successful life in terms of their relationships with other people. Their natural desire to understand the meaning of things enable them to finely attune to the experiences of others, and to provide valuable help to those in need. This is the earthly expression of divine love and the fulfilling of a karmic need common to all Sagittarians.

○ CAPRICORN – DECEMBER 23 TO JANUARY 21

Characteristic expression

Caution is the keynote of Capricornian expression. People born under this sign are generally intensely practical – too practical to take risks or attempt anything about which they have any reservations. Though they have the reputation for being determined, Capricorn people could not be truly regarded as having a strong general determination, but rather as being deliberate in doing those things that fall within the ambit of the conventionally acceptable. As exceptionally law-abiding citizens, they will not go beyond the commonly accepted limitations of conventional society. Consistent with their orthodox attitude to society, these people place great emphasis upon material security, talent and position. Many Capricornians are found at the head of large, established corporations, trusts and syndicates, where they serve very capably and faithfully. Children born when the sun is in Capricorn have very retentive memories, but unless they take steps to develop and train their memory, this valuable natural asset will dissipate soon after their academic studies have concluded. Another special aspect of these children is their need for peace – they have a deep inner urge for periods of solitude, without which they could become inexplicably melancholy. In fact, it is quite possible that some cot deaths are caused by undue noise shattering the delicate emotional balance of infants born under the sign of Capricorn – especially if they also possess the Arrow of Activity on their Birth Charts.

Negative tendencies to be surmounted

With the approach of the Aquarian age comes a changing pattern of values in society. The orthodox is being questioned, the conventional is being modified, and everything is being investigated as to its suitability for the New Age society. This is typically Aquarian, but very un-Capricornian. Consequently, many people born under the sign of Capricorn are currently feeling insecure because their deep faith in materialism is being shaken. This produces an uneasiness that worries them. From this confusion will come a necessary reawakening, a reassessment of their values. They will recognise the important differences between the human-made and the natural values in life, between the artificial and the real, the transient and the eternal. Until this realisation brings about the establishment of a new set of values, life will seem empty and they will experience much indefinable sadness. They can be easily helped when these causes are recognised, for then they will become aware of the need to adjust their outlook and to plan for the future, rather than live in the past.

Health aspects

Relating Capricorn to the anatomy of the human body, we find that its emphasis is directed toward the knees and legs. It is, therefore, in this region that special care must be exercised. Caution must be intensified if two or more 4s appear on the Birth Chart. The most abundant mineral salt in the human body is the most critical to the health of Capricornians. Cal Phos – calcium phosphate – is the bone-building material that is important to the health of everyone, but especially to those born under this sign. Most Capricornians are susceptible to weakened bones, bone and tooth decay (caries) and excessive albumin in their urine. This free albumin is unable to find sufficient calcium phosphate with which to combine and it consequently overflows into the urine for elimination. The chronic calcium phosphate deficiency symptom of thyroid enlargement, which causes the condition known as goitre, is not due to a lack of iodine but to excessive free albumin. Other calcium phosphate deficiency symptoms that might become evident from time to time are colds and tonsilitis, difficulty in swallowing, periods of hoarseness, head and face irritations, nervousness and lack of concentration. The orthodox outlook of Capricornians is nowhere more characteristically expressed than in their dietary habits. They follow unquestioningly the modern diet of refined and processed foods, abundant meat and white bread, tea and coffee, sweets and chocolates, and so on. In short, theirs is a diet of limited nutritional value, imposing upon their bodies undesirable acid residues, particularly uric and oxalic acids. Both these acids leach from the body vital stores of calcium phosphate, creating an inherent problem for people born under Capricorn. Foods affording valuable supplies of natural calcium phosphate are (in descending order of concentration):

- Yeast – brewer's and torula
- Swiss and cheddar cheeses
- All raw, unsalted nuts and seeds
- Soya beans, soya grits and soya milk
- Fresh, unprocessed wheatgerm
- Whey powder
- Fresh, raw egg yolks
- Parsley, broccoli and most other green vegetables, particularly sprouted

Karmic lesson

As an Earth sign, Capricorn indicates involvement in service to humankind. But first, spiritual understanding must be attained to expand the Capricornian outlook. Some find this through their church, some through service clubs, others through charitable work. It is a difficult challenge for Capricornians to recognise the limitations that a material frame of mind has. But this they must do it they are to triumph over their dogmatism. In addition, they must learn to develop a sensitivity and respect for other people's feelings, at least to the extent that they seek the same.

◦ AQUARIUS – JANUARY 22 TO FEBRUARY 20

Characteristic expression

As harbingers of the New Age, Aquarians, not surprisingly, focus on the quality of life and work for the betterment of all living creatures – humanity in particular. It is imperative to the Aquarian that they be allowed to study life in all its grandeur. Such a preoccupation embraces an extremely broad scope: science, philosophy, religion (comparative rather than orthodox), mathematics (applied rather than theoretical) and anything related to veneration for life. This is typically New Age. Fundamental to everything Aquarian is their need to be trusted, their need for truth and their abhorrence of hypocrisy. Every Aquarian has an interest in metaphysical concepts, which is only now being given full scope in face of humankind's increasingly widened horizons of understanding. As a result, the role of the Aquarian is gaining greater importance in society. Blessed with a good memory and a naturally strong fortitude, Aquarians have always been the seekers of esoteric knowledge; but now they are coming into their own powerful era when such knowledge is not only accepted, but actually sought after.

Negative tendencies to be surmounted

Arising from their intense dislike of deception and hypocrisy, Aquarians are apt to overreact against those whom they regard as guilty of such conduct. It is then that they must remind themselves that life is full of lessons and that the hypocrite, by perpetuating such a sin, has initiated their own karmic retribution, which will manifest as their appropriate lesson at precisely the right time. The Aquarian should be ever ready to offer compassionate guidance and brotherly love; an emotional reaction would result in their own karmic debt. The Aquarian suffers acutely from tensions, due to their highly sensitive nervous system and delicate digestive system. Frequent headaches are the usual consequence. Other symptoms of emotional tension include impaired blood circulation, depression and constant tiredness – all the result of enervation. Aquarians must recognise that their acute sensitivity is intended to facilitate the understanding of life (both physically and metaphysically). Along with this they must learn to protect themselves from those who would impose on them and waste their vital energy, or attempt to regulate and exploit their powers.

Health aspects

The expression of the Aquarian reveals itself more in mental and spiritual realms rather than the physical realm. They should, therefore, not try to emulate feats of physical prowess performed by others, but be content with their own special powers. Aquarians have certain vulnerable parts of their bodies that require special care. These are the ankles, calves and neck. It follows that they should avoid skiing, football and other sports or activities in which these parts of the body are placed in jeopardy. Aquarians generally have slender necks and will often register tension in this region, causing headaches or back pain requiring chiropractic care. The biochemic cell salt most needed by Aquarians is Nat Mur – sodium chloride. This is usually referred to as common salt and is the second most plentiful salt in the body. But the sodium chloride demanded by the body as a component of cellular nutrition is certainly not the common salt originating in seawater. Sea salt and table salt are far too coarse for the body's use because they irritate the highly sensitive linings of the gastrointestinal tract. Its addition to food will often lead to hypertension, swollen joints and other problems involving the blood and joints. We must obtain our basic nutrients from the soil of which out body originally derived, as the Bible tells us and science confirms. Natural foods rich in sodium chloride include (in the most abundant amounts) spouted seeds and fresh green vegetables, especially celery, beetroot and carrots. Also included in the list are dried figs, raisins and sultanas. For those who seek additional sources, egg yolk, brewer's yeast and molasses can be taken. Deficiency in natural sodium chloride can cause impaired digestion due to a lack of mucous, dry mouth and throat, irritation of the eyes and skin, chilblains and reduced vitality. Contrary to popular belief, cramps do not arise from inadequate sodium chloride but rather from sluggish circulation and/or excessive cellular toxicity. Ingesting salt tablets after excessive perspiration defeats the body's efforts to rid itself of this unwanted saline toxicity through its pores.

Karmic lesson

The role of the Aquarian as harbinger of the New Age is already well know. This is achieved through the building of a strong bond of kinship that unites all humankind in tolerant respect for the individual, for human society is a huge conglomeration of people of vastly different spiritual ages, karmic histories, geographical limitations, ethnic origins and religious conditionings. Total guidance can, therefore, never be achieved by a rigid, dogmatic plan. Human betterment will result only from understanding that, permits the best development of the individual. But the essential ingredient to this is sisterhood: the recognition that the ideal fraternity of the New Age is based on the harmonising of individual personalities for the upliftment of all.

○ PISCES – FEBRUARY 21 TO MARCH 20

Characteristic Expression

Some of the sweetest, kindest people put on Earth are born under the sign of Pisces. These people seem to possess a special talent for helping those in need, considerably assisted by their hypersensitive nature. They are very responsive to environmental influences and, therefore, should not knowingly expose themselves to hostile conditions. The loyalty, trustworthiness and generosity of a well-adjusted Piscean are obvious to all who know them. It is because they are so willing that they are easily imposed upon and should learn to guard against this. Pisceans should not assume that everyone is as trustworthy as they are. The natural loving sympathy of people born under the sign of Pisces makes them ideal healers. Whether the demand be of a physical, emotional or psychic nature, they will understand and provide the help where it is most needed. Again, they do not regard this quality as anything special, believing everyone to be so endowed. This illustrates the beautiful, natural modesty of the Piscean – an unusual quality in these years of acute ambitiousness. Dedicated to helping humankind, the efficient and industrious Pisceans tend to overlook the less worthy motives of many with fewer scruples. They must learn to sharpen their powers of assessment and to discriminate between those souls who really need their help and those who merely want it because it is easier than helping themselves.

Negative tendencies to be surmounted

The lack of sound judgement that characterised younger Pisceans must often be remedied by hurtful experiences. It seems unfortunate that their acute sensitivity has to be so harshly treated, but so essential are life's lessons that no other method will suffice. As they develop a little more confidence, Pisceans become prone to overanxiety about those in need. No matter how much they do to help, they are invariably troubled by the thought that they are not doing enough. This anxiety can become a real problem unless they adopt a more philosophical understanding, supported by adequate training in as many of the natural therapies as they can assimilate. Unless they secure sound training, in their enthusiasm to heal Pisceans could unwittingly dissipate their energies and become despondent. This could lead them to seek solace in drugs, alcohol or crime. Some suffer from long-term mental derangement as a result of many and repeated annoyances.

Health aspects

The bodily extremities of the Piscean are of pronounced importance: they have strong healing hands but weak feet. There is a powerful magnetic healing force natural to Pisceans that is capably transmitted through their hands. Their feet often cause them anguish from strains, sprains, fallen arches and the like, indicating they must take special care of these vital appendages. The biochemic cell salt indispensable to the health of Pisceans is Ferrum Phos – ferric (iron) phosphate. As iron attracts oxygen, this vital mineral salt revitalises the body by energising the blood. Simultaneously, it carries oxygen around the body for use in its every function. If insufficient oxygen is available in the blood, the body attempts to distribute the ratios as best it can. To do this, the blood motion (pressure) is increased. This creates higher-than-normal heat, often high enough to be called fever. Rather than treat this fever with suppressant drugs, the amount of ferric phosphate should be increased by ensuring that the diet comprises foods rich in this nutrient. If the correction is not undertaken, the more chronic problem of anaemia can result. Further symptoms of deficiency in ferric phosphate include depression, bleeding, inflammatory pains and congestion. This is such a vital salt that its deficiency affects the functioning of every part of the body. A wide choice of natural foods rich in ferric phosphate, listed in order of concentration, are:

- Yeast – brewer's and torula
- Pepitas (pumpkin seed kernels)
- Sunflower seed kernels, raw and sprouted
- Soya beans, soya grits and soya milk
- Wheatgerm and bran
- Fresh, raw nuts – especially almonds, pistachios and pine nut kernels
- Egg yolk – fresh, preferabley raw
- Sprouted seeds, pulses and grains

Karmic lesson

This sign is the one that offers most peace. Yet we are passing through what has been universally regarded as the Piscean Age without appearing to have achieved much peace in the world. Other quite tremendous factors, based on the human cravings for power and fame, seemed to intercede, placing greater demand upon the forthcoming Aquarian Age to improve the quality of life on Earth. Pisceans are destined to play a unique role in this endeavour, for they are eminently qualified to teach the world peace through understanding and trust. By the same token they are intended to bring peace to those sick people whose illnesses have hindered their eternal search for the inner self.

CHAPTER .13

The power of names

One of the most acknowledged sounds to people's ears is their name. Doubtless you have noticed that, no matter how noisy the surroundings, when someone calls your name, your attention is instantly diverted to them.

Our names have become a very important sound to us, whether it be our given names, pet names, nicknames, or whatever appellations we prefer to use. Actually, our names must be regarded as an adopted part of our personality and expression. A name is important because its vibrations become fused with our own. The term "vibration" implies to not only the audible wave frequencies but, even more broadly, the symbolic vibrations of the name as indicated by its numerological pattern. These vibrations exert an influence on our very personality and individuality.

Many people overlook the influence exerted by their name on the overall expression of their personality, but let us not dismiss this subject too hastily. Names are not given to us by chance or by accident. They attach themselves to us according to our need, though we are rarely aware of this. Parents will choose a name for their child guided by some preference. What created that preference? Nothing occurs by chance – there is always a reason, whether we are aware of it or not. Likewise, there is always a reason for those who change their name – often a far deeper reason than initially suspected. Numerologically, we can reveal that reason and, in so doing, we discover a deeper side to our personality.

Reasons for selecting names can occupy an entire book of fascinating reading. But we are more immediately in need of understanding the influence of our name as it now relates to our individuality. This will throw further light upon the discovery of the inner self.

The force exerted by names on the moulding of the personality will primarily depend upon the strength of the name and its relationship to the Ruling Number of the person. If they have a less-than-powerful birth date, the influence of their name will be far greater than if the reverse applied. This is particularly exemplified in the life of the sixteen president of the United States, Abraham Lincoln. His birth date (February 12, 1809) was not powerful, but his name gave the strength he needed to overcome personality weaknesses and achieve a lasting place in history. By contrast, a powerful birth date, such as December 27, 1935, and the name John will find very little influence exercised upon the personality of the name.

Irrespective of age, all people respond to some degree to the vibrations of their names. This response is greatest during the impressionable years of infancy and adolescence. Indeed, it can be of great help to children if parents are numerologically guided in their selection of the children's names. Names that are chosen for balanced power can be far more beneficial to the children than names with conflicting vibrations. Personalities will be more balanced if the name and birth date harmonise.

To assess the power of a name we must start by obtaining its numerological values. This is achieved by translating the letters of the name to their equivalent numbers using the following table:

1	2	3	4	5	6	7	8	9
A	B	C	D	E	F	G	H	I
J	K	L	M	N	O	P	Q	R
S	T	U	V	W	X	Y	Z	

There is no immediate need to memorise this table, for the numerical equivalent of each letter will become readily recognised with practice. As A is the first letter of the alphabet, it is equivalent to the first number of the numerical scale, the number 1. Each successive letter after A relates to the equivalent number following 1. So, B is equivalent to 2, C to 3, D to 4, and so on to the last letter of the alphabet.

At this point many people ask, "But how do these systems relate to each other?" Experience proves that relationships do exist between the alphabetical and numerical systems of every culture. However, first let us become totally familiar with this method in our native language. Then, if we have the time and patience, we can expand our knowledge to a numerological understanding of another language.

When analysing names we are concerned only with the used names. It is of little more than academic interest to analyse a given name or a family name if it is not used by the person. Even if a name is changed for professional or any other reasons, our interest lies in analysing whatever name is used in daily life. For instance, Allen might prefer to be called Al, William might prefer Bill and Samantha might prefer Sam.

In other instances people have been known to dislike their first name, preferring to be known by their middle name. Others might dislike both their first and middle names, preferring to be known only by the initials of both. This is popular in some of the southern states of the US where, for instance, a person called Jacob Benjamin might wish to be known simply as J. B. – we would then analyse JB as his first name.

The analysis of rejected names will often throw an interesting light on the personalities that rejected them, indicating the reason for the change. There might also be environmental reasons – the name associated with people, places or social attitudes that they dislike. These can also often be numerologically explained. It is always illuminating to compare the reason given by the people for the change with that revealed by numerological analysis.

Whatever the reasons given by those persons, it is clear that the name they use is the one we must analyse, for used names are living names and only living names have vibrational influence on the inner self.

Practice will reveal that a different degree of emphasis will exist between a person's used first name and their family name (surname). As a rule, the first name is used more in personal affairs, so it has greater impact on the personality. Family names are used more frequently in business or professional circles, hence their greater influence in these fields. These points should be recognised when the analysis is being made.

In translating the first name, middle name or a nickname to its numerological equivalent we adopt a simple method of separating the number of consonants from vowels. This enables us to easily obtain the totals of vowel numbers and consonant numbers separately. From the separate totals, we can gain an understanding of the name's influence on the personality in terms of its Soul Urge (vowels) and its Outer Expression (consonants). Then by adding these two totals we obtain the Ruling Number equivalent of the name, the Complete Name Number. Please note that a double first name (for example, Sally-Anne) or a hyphenated surname are to be analysed as one name.

Examples of the following three names will indicate how the upper line of numbers represents the vowels of each name. When totalled, these provide the Soul Urge Number. The lower line of numbers represents the consonants and, by their totals, the Outer Expression Number is obtained as shown:

```
1       1   1              3
A  B  R  A  H  A  M              26/8
   2  9     8     4           23/5

5     9  1     5              20/2
E  L  I  Z  A  B  E  T  H              43/7
   3     8  2     2  8        23/5


   6                         6
J  O  H  N                      20/2
1  8  5                     14/5
```

◦ SOUL URGE NUMBERS

In the same way the individual numbers of the birth date are added to obtain the Ruling Number, individual numbers of each vowel in a name are added to obtain the Soul Urge Number, as indicated by the vowel numbers in the three above examples. The Soul Urge Number of the name Abraham is 3; Elizabeth is 2; John is 6. This method is followed for each of the used names of a person.

Vowels are the soul of a word, its life, so to speak. Every trained singer, actor and speaker recognises this. It is therefore apparent that the vowel numbers of a person's name bear a close relationship to that person's inner feelings, the nature of which is discernible from the total number of the vowel numbers, known appropriately as the Soul Urge Number.

From the Soul Urge Number of a given name we learn some of the more subtle aspects of the individual's spiritual sensitivity, fortitude and drive. These can be expressed in a number of ways: through feelings, emotions, desires, fancies, and so on. The forms of expression will vary with each Soul Urge Number.

◦ *Soul Urge 1*

This appears only in names containing the single vowel "A": Ann, Jack, Jan and Chad. The need for individual freedom of expression is indicated here. The means by which this is to be achieved will be demonstrated best by the person's Ruling Number. In general, this Soul Urge Number implies a strong desire for freedom, viz. sufficient time to themselves, either to relax or undertake some kind of personal artistic expression.

○ *Soul Urge 2*

Representative names are Anna, Elizabeth, Adam and Oliver – vowel numbers total either 2 or 20. Here is an urge to do things in a balanced way so that harmony prevails in every expression. These are generally quite intuitive people, with a strong preference for the natural over the artificial. In their dealings with other people they are very fair and, by the same token, expect the same in return.

○ *Soul Urge 3*

Representative names are Amanda, Joanne and Samantha – vowel numbers total 3, 12 or 21. With its emphasis always anchored on the mental, 3 as a Soul Urge Number combines feeling with thinking and assessing. The result is generally a capable appraisal of people and situations. This can be highly beneficial in business and professional activities.

○ *Soul Urge 4*

Representative names are Stuart, Una, Angus and Paul – vowel numbers total either 4 or 13. When the practical 4 is expressed at the soul level it indicates that the individual has very orderly, conservative opinions on a wide range of spiritual and emotional subjects embracing religion, love, marriage and life in general. They are usually quite orthodox in outlook and not given to emotional outbursts.

◦ *Soul Urge* 5

Representative names are Mike, Shirley, Keith and Drew – vowel numbers total either 5 or 14. With its natural strength derived from its location on the Soul Plane, the occurrence of 5 as a Soul Urge Number indicates great depth of feeling and the need for freedom and acceptance, the better to express such feelings. Whatever the aspect of life involved, these people will invariably feel strong about it and will have their say regarding it (unless some strong inhibitions are present in the Birth Chart, such as the Arrow of Hypersensitivity).

◦ *Soul Urge* 6

Representative names are Charles, Allen, Megan and Jane – vowel numbers total either 6 or 15. Love and creativity are the operative words here. Every opportunity to express themselves creatively should be taken, whether at work, with a hobby or in the home. Their strength will decline into despair and torment if they lapse into overanxiety.

◦ *Soul Urge* 7

Representative names are Joan, Angela, Hamilton and Marianne – vowel numbers total either 7 or 16. The urge to teach and to help others is the predominant driving force here. However, they do not take too kindly to others teaching them, preferring to learn by their own experiences. They often pay dearly for this privilege until they come to the realisation that human beings are intended to help each other in a two-way relationship.

◦ *Soul Urge* 8

Representative names are Joanna, Bruce and Jonathan – vowel numbers total either 8 or 17. More then wishing to act inde-pendently, these people tend to mentally disassociate from unconventionally accepted habits, if such habits do not seem reasonable to them. They evidence a strong preference for individual thought and freedom but must guard against become aloof. One important lesson life teaches us is the need to participate in society without necessarily being bound by it.

○ *Soul Urge* 9

Representative names are Samuel, Claude and Jim – vowel numbers total 9 or 18. When living positively, these people always seek to improve the quality of life, guided by a keen sense of humanitarian responsibility. If living negatively, they tend to become overly ambitious, with an unbalanced idealism that nags them to engage in many egocentric (and often unsuccessful) acts. The power of this number should be respected and utilised altruistically, otherwise it can become a savage taskmaster.

○ *Soul Urge* 10

Representative names are Lisa, Craig, David and Douglas – vowel numbers total either 10 or 19. Metaphysical flexibility is the power conferred by this number. It offers the ability to bring into play a wide range of soul-oriented powers. Putting to use such metaphysical endowments as intuition, clairvoyance, clairaudience, thought transference and astral projection will negate many of the limitations society places on these people to suppress the expression of human individuality. To employ any of these faculties in daily life constructively emancipates these people from the earth-bound state and brings awareness of the divinity within human beings, the essence of life.

○ *Soul Urge* 11

Representative names are Robert, Errol and Cleo – vowel numbers total 11 only. The special spiritual qualities of the 11 are apparent here. As a Soul Urge Number, it offers a valuable intuitive strength that is especially beneficial if the individual does not have intuitive strength indicated on the Birth Chart, or as part of their Ruling Number. It also serves to increase compassion, an ability to attune to other people's feelings.

○ HOW TO ANALYSE THE "Y"

Numerologically, the Y is usually considered a consonant, with the value of 7. It will ordinarily appear as an Outer Expression Number, exemplified in such names as Kelly, Sally and Shirley. However, the exception arises in a name in which the Y is pronounced as "I" or "E" with no actual vowel appearing in the name. Then, and only then, do we analyse the Y as a vowel, thereby giving the name a Soul Urge Number of 7, as in Lyn and Ty, or the surnames Byrd, Hynd and Lynch.

○ OUTER EXPRESSION NUMBERS

Obtaining the value of the Outer Expression Number of each name follows the same pattern already established for Soul Urge Numbers. By adding together the numerical values of the consonants below the name (as shown in the examples), their total is obtained then easily converted to its single digit equivalent, which we now recognise as the Outer Expression Number. We find that each of the three names used in the examples has, coincidentally, an Outer Expression Number of 5.

The Soul Urge Numbers range from 1 through to 11. The same holds true for the Outer Expression Numbers, except for the additional number of 22/4. Experience has shown that names in the English language possess insufficient vowels to total 22; however, it is not uncommon to find names with consonants that give this total.

Characteristics associated with each of the Outer Expression Numbers are:

○ Outer Expression 1

This can only occur with names that have the single consonant of J or S. Few given names comply with this limitation but among those that do, Sue and Joe are the most commonly used. The trait most notably expressed by this number is exemplified by the solo sportsperson or solo worker. They are the people who need the freedom to set their own pace in order achieve greatest satisfaction and to develop their self-confidence in physical activities.

○ Outer Expression 2

Examples of names are Samantha, Jose and Nicholas – names with consonant number totals of either 2 or 20. Indicated here is the preference to work as part of a group in happy surroundings. They are bright people with a desire for fun and lighthearted pleasures. This does not imply that they are shallow, but rather that they have a great capacity to enjoy organised activity.

○ Outer Expression 3

Examples of names are Sacha, Keith, Jody and Beth – names with consonant number totals of 3, 12, 21 or 30. Whereas the Outer Expression Number of 2 reveals a person who enjoys being entertained, the 3 reveals the person as an entertainer. They derive great pleasure, and give as much to others, by being the life of the party, for they usually have a quick wit and a bright outlook.

○ Outer Expression 4

Examples of names are Eloise, Ada, Rod and Angus – names with consonant number totals of 4, 13 or 31. This is an intensely practical number that belongs to doing people who always seek involvement with their hands, feet or bodies. They specifically enjoy sports and building or repairing things.

○ Outer Expression 5

Examples of names are Dianna, Andrew, Stuart and Rachel – names with consonant number totals of 5, 14, 23 or 32. Freedom from physical confinement is the oft-expressed need of these people. Yet they sometimes allow misunderstandings or shyness to inhibit the fullness of their expression. To avoid such frustration they should seek job that does not confine them, and the company of those with whom they feel at ease – to put it simply, they need the company of responsive, uninhibited people.

○ Outer Expression 6

Examples of names are James, Jane, Douglas and Angela – names with consonant number totals of 6, 15, 24 or 33. The tendency to focus much of their energies and attention on the home is the ever present characteristic here. Of course, this might appear to have very decided advantages for the family, but it can also spoil them. Caution must be used to avoid over-indulgence by maintaining a practical balance between pampering and attending to the more realistic needs of the domestic circle.

○ Outer Expression 7

Examples of names are Oliver, Philip and Megan – names with consonant number totals of 7, 16, 25 or 34. These people have the compulsion to do things themselves, being strongly motivated toward personal involvement and learning on their own terms and in their own way. They much prefer a personal sense of achievement and the satisfaction of discovering for themselves the more amenable course of learning from others.

○ *Outer Expression* 8

Examples of names are Adam, Samuel and Bill – names with consonant number totals of 8, 17, 26 or 35. We find here a very strong desire for independent expression. These are people who elect to act individually, to the extent that they dare to be different if the need demands it. In this manner they assert their strong personalities, for they are aware that humans can never achieve a high level of self-development when identified with the herd mind.

○ *Outer Expression* 9

Examples of names are Sarah, Pat and Don – names with consonant totals of 9, 18, 27 or 36. There is no denying that life has its serious and its humorous sides. A balanced personal life is one in which the two successfully interrelate. Unhappily, people with this Outer Expression Number tend to over-emphasise the seriousness of life. In so doing they attract sadness and sometimes loneliness, the result of not considering the lighter side of life to be of sufficient importance. Their capacity for deep contemplation and penetrative analysis, and for the implementation of their high ideals, are fine virtues, but they must be balanced with a little light pleasure to revitalise the mind and body.

○ *Outer Expression* 10

Examples of names are Craig, Paul, Shirley, Claude and Ann – names with consonant number totals of 10, 19, 28 or 37. Outer expression traits indicated by this number are virtually the opposite of those applying to the 9. The inclination to guard against here is that of becoming too flippant and superficial, when the real function of the number is adaptation to life's varying circumstances and situations. People with this Outer Expression Number should be prepared to exert greater determination to fulfil their role in life, for only by balancing seriousness with lightness will they achieve success.

○ *Outer Expression* 11

Examples of names are Allen, Joanne, Kara and Jonathan – names with consonant number totals of either 11 or 29. The predominant need here is for harmony. Balanced emotional and spiritual expression is indicated by this Outer Expression Number. Its special purpose is to instil a desire in themselves and others to harmonise surroundings, control emotions and develop and share a deepened understanding of life. It is only by following this path that the individual will be led through the gates of happiness.

○ *Outer Expression* 22/4

Examples of names are Hamilton and Robert – those few names with a consonant number total of 22 only. We know this to be an exceptionally strong power for organising, especially in business and commercial ventures. If the person's Ruling Number is a 4, 8 or 22/4, special care must be taken to maintain balance, for the strong leaning here is towards an over-emphasis on moneymaking, almost to the point of obsession. Even for people with other Ruling Numbers, the same advice will apply: endeavour to expand your organisational skills into other than commercial fields by working in such compassionate fields as worthy charities, particularly those benefiting under-privileged children, if you wish to gain equilibrium.

○ COMPLETE NAME NUMBERS

The third aspect of the numerology of names is the key to the name's general strength. This is known as the Complete Name Number. It is related to, but less powerful than, the Ruling Number.

The Complete Name Number is obtained by adding together all the numbers of a name, then totalling them in the same way as was done to obtain the Ruling Number. (Remember to use the name you most identify with, whether that be your first name, a nickname, a middle name, or a new name you've chosen to adopt.)

Complete Name Numbers range in value from 2 through to 11 and then 22/4. The extent of the influence of the Complete Name Number lies in its relationship to the Ruling Number, rather than any specific contribution of its own. A Complete Name Number can either balance or reinforce the power of the Ruling Number. If it is numerically the same as the Ruling Number, it offers the greatest reinforcement to the Ruling Number. If the Complete Name Number is different to the Ruling Number, but both are on the same Plane (4, 7 and 10 on the Physical Plane; 2, 5, 8 and 11 on the Soul Plane; 3, 6 and 9 on the Mind Plane; and 22/4 both on the Physical and Soul Planes), then balancing reinforcement is given on that Plane.

Finally, if a Complete Name Number is on a different plane to the Ruling Number, a wider range of vibrations is provided for the broadening of the personality.

○ NAMECHART

Analysing the Soul Urge, Outer Expression and Complete Name Numbers of people's names will provide an understanding of some of the post-natal influences that the name provides. A chart of the name, similar to that drawn up for the birth date, will unveil further aspects of its contribution to the development of the personality.

The number equivalent of the name's individual letters is placed in its correct space on the chart to show the pattern of the name. To illustrate we shall use the three sample names of Abraham, Elizabeth and John, and construct the Name Charts.

$$
\begin{array}{ccccccc}
1 & & & 1 & & 1 & \\
A & B & R & A & H & A & M \\
& 2 & 9 & & 8 & & 4
\end{array}
\qquad
\begin{array}{cccccccc}
5 & 9 & & 1 & & 5 & & \\
E & L & I & Z & A & B & E & T & H \\
& 3 & 8 & & 2 & & 2 & 8
\end{array}
\qquad
\begin{array}{cccc}
& & 6 & \\
J & O & H & N \\
1 & & 8 & 5
\end{array}
$$

		9
2		8
111	4	

3		9
22	55	88
1		

	6	
	5	8
1		

The name patten is a distinct help in more fully evaluating the personality. When we place the Name Chart beside the Birth Chart, we look for the relationship between the.

Close examination of the juxtaposed Name and Birth Charts shows that there are three possibilities to look for:

o Does the Name Chart offer any strengths that balance weaknesses on the Birth Chart? This is the most desirable function of the Name Chart. For instance, if the Birth Chart had the Arrow of Hypersensitivity (numbers 2, 5 and 8) and the Name Chart had the Arrow of Emotional Balance (2, 5 and 8), then we have the most desirable balance. If the Name Chart only had one or two numbers on the Soul Plane this could still provide some valuable balance.

o Does the Name Chart intensify any strength already present on the Birth Chart? This creates the most undesirable combination. For instance, if the Name Chart had any of the same arrows as the Birth Chart, or if it had an abundance of the same numbers as those already appearing on the Birth Chart, there would be too great a concentration of strength. Wherever you have an over concentration of power you will always find compounded weakness – balance is much more desirable. Remember that the Birth Chart cannot be changed, but the name can. In these instances it is wise to look to a modification in the structure of the name to try to provide better balance.

○ Does the name do nothing for the Birth Chart? From time to time this predicament presents itself. This occurs when a Name Chart cannot offer significant strength to balance weaknesses on the Birth Chart, or when the same weaknesses prevail on both charts. In either case the name is providing neither advantage nor disadvantage. Yet often, with a slight change in spelling, alteration in length or interchange of names, definite advantages can develop to provide harmony and balance. Alternatively, a total name change should be considered.

To illustrate with an easy-to-follow example, we shall take one of the names previously used as an illustration, and the birth date of a person suited – Queen Elizabeth II, born April 21, 1926.

BIRTHCHART

$$2+1+4+1+9+2+6= 25/7$$

	6	9
22		
11	4	

NAMECHART

```
5   9   1   5           20/2
E L I Z A B E T H        4:
3   8   2   2 8          23/5
```

3		9
22	55	88
1		

PYRAMIDS

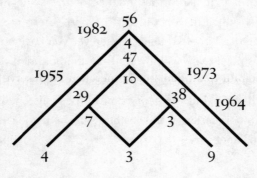

The most noticeable similarity is that her Ruling Number and Complete Name Number are both 7. This strengthens the Ruling Number, indicating the need to undergo many personal sacrifices in early years in order to attain a level of adjustment and self-control, as well as an ability to impart guidance to others.

The plane of strongest expression here is the Spiritual Plane. It indicates balanced intuition and sensitivity (the two 2s on the Birth Chart supported by a doubling of the Arrow of Emotional Balance on the Name Chart). Further spiritual strength comes from the Soul Urge and Outer Expression Numbers of the name (2 and 5 respectively), as they are both spiritual numbers.

The Mind Plane of the Queen's Birth Chart is also strong and well-balanced, for though it is devoid of the 3 it is compensated for by her Day Number 3. Added mental balance is indicated by the top line of her Name Chart.

Her combination of mental and spiritual balance, together with her capacity for self-expression (as indicated by the two 1s on her Birth Chart), disclose her natural ease in communicating just what and how much she wishes to reveal (the double Arrow of Emotional Balance on the Name Chart), but her Ruling Number 7 and Complete Name Number 7 indicate that she had much to learn about what should and should not be said in public. She found such conforming difficult because she felt that it curtailed her freedom.

No arrows of strength appear on her Birth Chart. However, her strongest inherent guidance derives from her intuition. This is reinforced by the two 2s on her Name Chart which are at the centre of the Arrow of the Planner.

It will be helpful to students of numerology to observe some further points of importance regarding Queen Elizabeth's personality:

o Ruling 7 people are usually among the most truthful and honest to be found. This virtue is especially apparent here, for Queen

Elizabeth takes her position as "protector of the faith" very seriously, employing uncompromising sincerity to try to live up to the ethics of her church. Hypocrisy is abhorrent to her, hence the conflicts within her family must have upset her greatly. Such disharmony is felt very deeply by the Queen due to her strong sense of family responsibility (indicated by the 6 and 9 together without a 3 on her Birth Chart).

○ So many factors about the Queen's charts and pyramids indicate that life to her is a very serious business. She has little time or patience with flippancy. Her strong Soul Plane and the numbers about the Peaks of her Pyramids show that she is a person who would never shirk her responsibilities. In fact, the 9 as the last number on the base of her pyramids indicates that she has even more responsibilities to face in the final stage of her life – the Fulfilment.

○ Her alert intuition (the double 2s) combined with the Ruling Number 7 and Complete Name Number 7 is a very reliable indicator of her approach to making decisions. No doubt many of the Queen's advisers have complained that she does not consult them as often as she should. In her mind she does not need to, and now that she has passed the third Peak of her Pyramids, her maturity is so well developed that she could probably be of more guidance to her advisers than they to her.

○ The doubling of the 1s and 2s on her Birth Chart indicate how capably the Queen can appreciate other people's viewpoints. She can readily comprehend both sides of a contentious matter – an important attribute when dealing so much with public figures, especially politicians.

○ The seriousness of her regal position occupies so much of Queen Elizabeth's thoughts that she needs encouragement to allow some diversion into her life. Prince Philip, with his highly developed sense of humour, is especially helpful in this regard. With his encouragement, the Queen does not take long to discover her "other" self through her Day Number 3. The further influence of her Outer Expression Number 5 reveals that she has the ability to enjoy light entertainment and desires to be free to indulge in that enjoyment from time to time.

o An analysis of Prince Philip's name and date of birth (June 10, 1921) provides an excellent exercise for the student. From this it can be seen how much dedicated support he has given the Queen and how much it has assisted her to ease so graciously into her high position in public life. It will also become clear how well suited the Queen and her husband are. Without his support, her acute sensitivity could have led Queen Elizabeth to become somewhat withdrawn.

This is not intended to be an exhaustive analysis, but rather an indication of the interrelationship between the various aspects of numerology. The Queen was chosen as an example because of her worldwide fame and single name. Under normal circumstances we have at least two names to analyse for a person (the first name and surname). If they are in show business or have taken a pseudonym for professional reasons, we must also analyse those to ascertain the relationships between the various names as well as the birth date characteristics.

o CHOOSING A SUITABLE NAME

From the foregoing analysis it is clear how helpful the name Elizabeth is to the Queen. When we analyse successful people we find this to be a consistent fact: almost without exception, their name will be in harmony with, and a source of strength to, their natal powers.

How does a couple go about choosing a name for a newborn babe? Rarely does a person consider it necessary to consult a numerologist to have desirable names analysed, yet such a practice would greatly assist development of the child's individuality by creating more harmony between the natal characteristics and those of the name.

In practice, we find some surprisingly inspired instances of parents who unconsciously chose ideal names for their children. It is as though they were strongly impressed to choose such names by some power of which they had little or no cognizance. Unfortunately, all too often we find that people have names that create something short of ideal harmony or balance for their personality. Some people have themselves recognised this problem and have changed their used name with subsequent success. This often occurs in the acting and literary professions.

Some years ago, an attractive young woman came to me for advice on how she could improve her acting and so get better parts in films, TV series and plays. She had heard that it was numerologically possible to change one's name to bring about "better luck," as she called it. Up until then, she had only managed to get work in TV commercials, but she so wanted to play romantic roles in dramatic shows.

An analysis of her numerology revealed that a key aspect of her problem was the Arrow of Hypersensitivity on her Birth Chart, with no counteracting strength from either her Ruling Number (which was 6), her Name Chart, or Soul Urge and Outer Expression Numbers. This inhibited her emotional expression.

The remedy was to advise her of a name change. In so doing, I had her choose alternative stage names that felt comfortable to her. From the list she gave me on the next visit, I chose one that stood out clearly as offering her an improved balanced expression for her sensitivity in conjunction with the vibrant creative power offered by her Ruling 6. She liked the new name and immediately began to use it professionally. Within a month, she got an important role in a new romantic TV drama. It was not the lead, but soon after she got an unexpected lead role in a play.

As people become more aware of the important role of the name in their life, they will seek guidance in the wise selection of a name. With increasing frequency, numerologists are being consulted to advise on suitable names for professionals, as well as newborn babies, businesspeople, or even people who find that life is not as kind to them as they feel it should be.

When considering the acceptability of a name for a person or for an organisation, we take into account the following factors:

o The name should provide balance to the Birth Chart by supplying strengths on the Name Chart where there are weaknesses on the Birth Chart. This helps the person to overcome their natal weaknesses.

o Where strengths appear on the Birth Chart, the Name Chart should not compound the same power to create an overbalance of too much strength in a particular direction.

o The Name Chart should not have the same arrows as the Birth Chart as this will not make for balance.

These points are clearly shown in the following examples:

Keith, born July 16, 1963

7+1+6+1+9+6+3 = 33/6

$$
\begin{array}{cccc}
 & 5 & 9 & \\
\text{K} & \text{E} & \text{I} & \text{T} & \text{H} \\
2 & & & 2 & 8
\end{array}
$$

14/5
26/8
12/3

3	66	9
11		7

		9
22	5	8

The great emphasis indicated by the Birth Chart on the mental level is accentuated by the Ruling Number. The major weakness is obviously in the spiritual (feeling) area, indicated by the Arrow of Hypersensitivity. Choosing the name Keith is a great help to this child's sensitivity, providing balance by the addition of the Arrow of Emotional Balance on the Name Chart. Further help comes from the Complete Name Number (8), and the Soul Urge Number (5), both of which are feeling numbers. At the same time there is minimal mental emphasis contributed by the name, thereby avoiding overbalance in this direction. In conclusion, it would be hard to think of a more suitable name than Keith for the child born with the birth date of July 16, 1963.

Charles, born September 7, 1974

1+2+7+1+9+7+4=31/4

		1		5		6	
C	H	A	R	L	E	S	30/3
3	8		9	3		1	24/6

		9
2		
11	4	77

		9
33		
	5	8
11		

With a ruling number of 4 and with such a heavy weight of power on the Practical Plane of the Birth Chart, it is wise to avoid a Name Number of 1, 4, 7 or 10, or overweighing the Practical Plane of the Name Chart with too many numbers. Charles is fitting here as it adds only two 1s in the practical area. More significantly, such a name provides great mental strength to compensate for its absence in the Birth Chart. The Name Chart provides all the numbers that are missing on the Birth Chart, except 6. However, 6 appears in the name as both the Soul Urge Number and Outer Expression Number. An extremely unsuitable name for this child would be David. As an exercise, analyse it and see just how strong it is on the Practical Plane. Notice also how it over-balances the individual's power in an extremely materialistic direction, with so little on the Soul and Mind Planes to compensate.

◦ ADVICE TO PARENTS

There are many advantages to patiently waiting until babies have arrived before choosing their first names. Though it is wise to have a selection of desirable names ready, it is unwise to make the final choice until the day of the birth. Not until then will the natal characteristics of the child be able to be analysed numerologically.

Encouraging the patient parents to prepare a short list of acceptable names has many advantages. The resultant names will, in a very subtle way, project harmony to the parents. This is highly important, for the parents must feel at ease with the names they are to call their children or they will not use them – then they will have no influence. Choosing a short list of names also gives the parents the opportunity to express their personal preference and, naturally, all parents want to do that. A third advantage of the short list is the time it saves the numerologist. Analysing hundreds of names to select one or two suitable ones is a tedious and time-consuming task.

Sometimes compromises have to be reached between numerologically ideal names and those that are pleasing to the ears of mother and father. For instance, if the parents of the child born on December 7, 1974 express a pronounced dislike for the name Charles, then it is not to be considered. If they do not like a suggested name, no matter how ideal its numerological value, when it is unused the value is negated.

The chosen names cannot be abbreviated without impairing the numerologist's work. If the parents of the previous example agree to the name Charles and then shorten it to Charley or Chas, an important part of its value is missing. The parents must be fully prepared to use the complete name if it is chosen. Otherwise, it would be more desirable to analyse and choose, if suitable, the abbreviated name. Perhaps the full name could then be used for formal purposes.

There are many occasions when people are given a formal name that is seldom used. Bill, for example, bears no relationship numerologically or phonetically to William, nor does Dick to Richard. These factors must be considered and the intended abbreviation or nickname always analysed. If suitable, its formal counterpart can still be used for the christening and the birth certificate – but remember, it has no influence unless it is used in everyday communication.

○ CHANGING A NAME

We all know people who have disliked their first name. At school, children have preferred to accept some nickname or abbreviated name given to them by classmates. Later in life a person may decide to formally change his or her first name for personal or professional reasons. Whatever the reason, a change in name will gradually produce some corresponding change in the personality.

Many unknown yet talented people have been known to change their name/s as a prelude to achieving notable success in the arts – particularly in music and acting. Such examples have been commonplace in Hollywood for as long as Hollywood has been the movie capital of the world. Among the examples is Clark Gable, whose first name was actually William.

In the world of music name changes are not unusual. Leopold Stokowski's surname was Stanislaw before he became one of the most famous orchestral conductors of this century. Dame Nellie Melba, born Helen Mitchell, became the most famous soprano in the world during the early part of this century.

Name changes in the literary world are not less numerous. Author Lewis Carroll was born Charles Lutwidge Dodgson; Mark Twain was born Samuel Clemens; French dramatist Jean Molière was born Jean Poquelin; Russian novelist Maxim Gorki was born Aleksey Maximovich Pyeshkov. It seems to be an international habit of long standing.

The observant student will note here that probably not one of the people mentioned sought the guidance of a numerologist when they changed their names. In most cases it is safe to say they were changes guided by their own intuition. And we know that genuine intuition is probably the most reliable form of guidance. But today, with so many experts offering opinions and so many entertainment agencies flooding our consciousness with rubbish, our psychic powers are often unable to flow freely and we are very much in need of accurate, reliable and scientific guidance. This is where numerology proves its value.

More and more often, people seek the advice of numerologists regarding their names. Artists, composers, writers and even students have all been clients of mine over the past two decades. One very memorable occasion was when a budding young painter sought guidance regarding a name change. He was experiencing failure after frustrating failure as an artist. After consultation, we decided to change his name, and he liked it so much (and the method of selecting it) that he immediately enrolled in my forthcoming twelve week numerology course. By the time the course was scheduled to start two months later, he had so many commissions to paint for exhibitions that he had no time to attend the lectures.

It is not that the change in name will necessarily alter an artist's style. Instead its benefit lies in allowing such a slight modification to the personality that one feels as though a trigger has been released and some small inhibition swept aside, permitting the expression to flow freely. Such a minor factor in the personality is often the only barrier between success and mediocrity.

Reasons for changing names are not limited to artists. How many kings, queens, princes, dukes, earls, lords and others associated with royalty undertake name changes? The most famous of all modern royal name changes was that undertaken by the British Royal House in 1917. From its Germanic origins of Saxe-Coburg-Gotha came the House of Windsor. Many reasons are given in history for such a dramatic name change, but numerologically we can see that it was not such a wise move. Windsor is strong in determination and in willpower, but it is a weak name in terms of planning, action and expression of ideals in comparison to the previous longer name. So we wonder: was it coincidental that this same period of history saw the start of the decline in British superiority and worldwide political and cultural dominance?

Back further in time, we find a change of name to be instrumental in the development of Christianity. Observe in Genesis 17 of the Bible perhaps the two most important name changes in history: Abraham at 100 years of age was told to change his name from Abram; his wife, Sarah, at 90, was told to change her name from Sarai, and that is so doing their union would bring forth a child (Isaac).

Perhaps this practice might be considered by childless couples today. To change a name is to change something of the personality. Since a wise change is based on the removal of emotional blockages, its chances of success could be surprisingly high.

○ NAME CHANGES IN MARRIAGE

In these days of striving for equality of the sexes, we might ask why it is that the wives are the ones who must change name in marriage. The answer seems to be tradition. So far as the scientific aspect of name changing is concerned, it is of minor importance as to who actually changes the name in marriage, so long as one partner does.

As well as love, marriage must depend for its success on under-standing, trust and harmony between the partners. The challenge is to find harmony in the quickest, most permanent way. This is one of the most difficult adjustments people have to make in life, yet it is one that succeeds to an impressively high degree. When two newly-married people settle down to share the same home, meals and lifestyle, they find it involves far more than sharing the same bed or merely living together as single partners for a time. The difference lies in the marriage ceremony and, most important-ly, in sharing the same surname.

Unmarried couples who have lived together for some time before deciding to marry are always at a loss to explain the differ-ences in their attitudes that emerge after the ceremony. Adjusting to this new state, even though they lived together beforehand, can be quite demanding. But as their personalities draw more closely together, adjustment becomes easier, facilitated to a great extent by the sharing of the same family name.

Hollywood-style marriages seem unique in that they possess a record for the highest failure rate. Partners of such marital unions are so often acting as other personalities that they lose contact with their own inner self, without which they cannot discover the real meaning of love. By maintaining their pre-marriage names, these people resist the unifying influence of sharing a common surname, one of the primary requirements for a successful marriage. It is impossible to become part of a successful marital union and still maintain total independence.

By now it must be apparent that people's names are not merely sounds used to attract someone's attention. In using them, sets of vibrations are energised that exert varying degrees of influence upon their owners. We are equipped now to gauge the nature and extent of such influences, and it benefits us to use the power of names with wisdom and care.

CHAPTER .14

Compatibilities in relationships

*P*hysical appearance often attracts two people together and gradually love develops between them. Some are drawn together by instant love that seems to set bells ringing in each other's hearts. Yet other couples are drawn together by a mutual admiration for each other's minds or souls. Regardless of the love story that highlights your relationship, there are firm guidelines by which couples continue to live together in love, peace and mutual benefit for almost endless years.

Some love relationships are older than the two participants themselves, their roots buried deep in the karmic histories of each person. Other unions are destined to far exceed the current lives of each of the lovers. But for a love relationship to succeed it must be firmly anchored in far more than either physical attraction or mental stimulation.

Remember, humans are tripartite beings. We have three Selves to nourish and the ideal relationship does just that. Physically, each person needs to stimulate and nourish the other's emotions; mentally, each needs to excite and expand the other's knowledge and awareness of life; and spiritually, they need to share a deep love and compassion for each other and life. We need to meet and harmonise on all three Planes if a true and lasting love is to sustain a relationship.

As a marriage guidance counsellor and consultant nutritionist, I found that many people who came to see me with problems in one of these areas invariably discovered how both areas are intimately related. Without the vital aid of numerology, this discovery and ways to rectify it might have required many consultations to be resolved, instead of merely one or two visits.

With numerology at our disposal, we are equipped with a laser technique for honing into the very core of the situation to understand and unravel its complexities with accuracy. These complexities are invariably far deeper and more intricate than the clients would have believed possible, as the following real life example indicates.

The couple that sat opposite me in my consulting room seemed happy enough. Ostensibly, they came to see me to resolve their health problems – everything else in their lives was fine they said. When they described their diet to me, I could find no major problem with what they were regularly eating, yet he had just recovered from a mild heart attack, while she had chronic indigestion accompanied by halitosis. My intuition told me I was not getting the full story.

After setting up their complete Birth Charts, I became immediately aware of the deeper problem. Here were two people who had shared the marriage home for over 40 years, had successfully raised three children (themselves now married), were financially secure with a comfortable suburban home, and yet they were so different.

They had learned to adjust to each other on a superficial level appeared to enjoy the same tastes and pleasures but deep down, each felt somewhat unfulfilled in so many other areas of their lives. His fervent desire for peace induced him to compromise in most matters, a habit she came to expect. Neither was prepared to acknowledge the real differences that existed between them; that is, until I explained exactly what appeared in their respective numerology charts. And then it happened. He started quietly sobbing. She followed.

The next half hour was one of astounding revelation for them both. He was born 9/1/1930, she 5/5/1932. He was a Ruling Number 5, she an 8. He had the Arrows of Hypersensitivity and Frustration, she had the Arrow of Determination. He had two 1s, she had one 1. She also had two 5s to compound her indigestion (though they did not create the cause).

His frustration at being inhibited from freely expressing himself (revealed by his two weak arrows and her intense determination) and her difficulty at being able to fluently express her deep inner feelings (revealed by her one 1) contributed to his heart attack. His problem was compounded by this isolated ego expression and idealism (two 1s and two 9s unconnected). He also needed ample freedom to express himself emotionally (Ruling 5), whereas she needed his close dependability and did not find it easy to be as loving as he needed (her negative Ruling 8 aspects).

They learned a lot about themselves and each other through their numerology charts and were able, in time, to make some important adjustments. Within a month they called to report "amazing results." Her indigestion had vanished, as had her bad breath, his breathing had improved, and they were planning their first overseas holiday together in ten years.

It is not always possible or wise to discuss the details of your numerological findings about someone to them at the time. Yet, so much better if this can be done, for it gives credence to why and how you discovered so much about your clients in such a brief time. Open-minded people never fail to be surprised at what numerology can reveal, especially where human relationships are concerned. And, thankfully, more and more open-mindedness is developing in the community. If clients are totally open-minded, you can even go into the karmic explanation of why they are together, thereby guiding them a step further in their understanding (see Chapter 16).

Very often we find married couples brought together for reasons that seem far deeper than merely for the pleasure of physical and mental intercourse. We never cease to be amazed, upon numerologically analysing the birth dates of many married couples, at the disharmony in their basic characteristics and personalities. Yet they seem to be very much in love. Obviously, marriage has much more to teach us in the delicate art of personality adjustment and self-discovery than we can discern from the bed or the dining table. Even so, the guidance available to us for expediting these changes can significantly reduce the "adjustment period" that follows the honeymoon, bringing understanding sooner. And nothing can achieve this as quickly or accurately as numerology.

With so much to learn in life, we have usually reached maturity before gaining sufficient understanding of ourselves to wisely select a compatible marriage partner. For many people, this does not occur until the second or third marriage. Young people about to marry are often too headstrong and brash to be guided by older and wiser counsel, and too immature to consider the importance of employing such accurate means of self-analysis as that provided by numerology.

A marriage partnership is the most important association we establish in life. So we should be far more conscious of it than to believe that emotional love is the only prerequisite. But total love – spiritual, mental and physical – is another matter. Without it a marriage will not last.

Many people marry in anticipation of discovering love, or they hope to have the love of their intended to satisfy their own lack of it. This does not auger well for a solid relationship. The ideal marriage is based on each partner having individually found deep, inner love and feeling so attuned to it that they seek to share it.

Basically, there are two types of relationship: the supplementary and the complimentary. Our use of these two classifications makes rather liberal use of the words, but it is important to realise the difference and recognise the types of marriages to which they refer.

The supplementary marriage is one where the opposites prevail – the weaknesses of the one partner are negated by the same traits being strengths in the other partner and vice versa. These people are constantly finding exciting differences in each other and are constantly learning and strengthening their individual characteristics from the exchange. Karmic relationships fall within this category. More long-term marriages exist in this group, characterised by each partner having many separate interests from the other.

Complimentary marriages are those where the two participants have very similar characteristics. They are attracted by their similarities, but these can wear thin after some years. Such marriages need considerable stimulation to keep them exciting and avert the boredom that might otherwise take over. The partners generally share similar interests and it is in this area where the marriage either survives or fails. In fact, it is in these marriages where numerological guidance can be the most beneficial, for it assists the partners to develop aspects of their individuality they did not realise existed, deviating from those similarities upon which they have been constantly focusing. No matter how similar two people are, significant differences can always be discovered that enable them to expand into areas of expression they have not previously contemplated. This is specially so in the case of "identical" twins.

CHAPTER .15

Developing Intuition & ESP. using numerology

Numerology is an intensely practical system designed to provide a unique insight into human personality and its potential, but it is much more than that. It is a valuable means whereby our intuition and extrasensory perception (ESP) can develop and, in turn, improve all-round psychic awareness. Such awareness extends beyond physical limitations.

Everyone has the paraphysical senses of ESP and intuition. However, not everyone is aware of these. Preoccupation with the physical tends to hamper the awakening of such consciousness. Gradually, through repeated flashes of insight, we become aware that it is possible to attain knowledge of an event before it actually happens. This is an intuitive skill. On other occasions, we become conscious of other people's thought, or of conflicts in their emotional make-up. These we detect through our extrasensory perception.

Intuition is a very comprehensive sense. In popular usage it is a word employed to cover any sense of feeling beyond the ordinary that might be interpreted as a personal guide. This is rather inaccurate because it tends to confuse intuition and ESP. Though these two senses are closely related, they have very definite fields of application. Intuition comes before thought. It manifests itself in momentary flashes only because thought takes over. Thought then either accepts and develops the intuitive impulse, or else rationalises and rejects it. The selection is determined by our conditioning.

On the other hand, ESP depends on the user being in a state of relaxation. This allows the mind to be extended and projected to other sources of vibration, particularly human, though it also encompasses spiritual, animal, mineral and plant energy fields. (A source of vibration creates around itself an energy field that reveals the essence and quality condition of that source.) Having met with a particular energy field the mind transmits the impressions back to the brain; the brain translates these into comprehensible terms.

In practice we find the general term of intuition covers such faculties as first impressions, foreknowledge, premonitions and pre-conceptions. These invariably must be accepted on faith, for they can rarely be rationalised. Extending into a further dimension, ESP depends on the mind's engagement of the brain to interpret the impressions. ESP includes clairvoyance, clairaudience, psychometry and mental telepathy.

The most important aspects of ESP insofar as numerology is concerned, is its value in detecting powerful prevailing vibrations. Extrasensory perception is both a guide and a protector. With its ability to perceive strong sources of energy it acts as a alarm bell, warning of harmful emotional turbulence created by such reactions as anger, hatred and lust. This indicates to the experienced numerologist critical problem areas for correction. Through its telepathic faculties, ESP also provides a means of mental contact with the subject being analysed, a contact that is crystallised when the person's numerological pattern is established through their Birth Chart.

In our pristine state, metaphysical senses were our means of being alerted to anything that might endanger our safety; they also provided us with constructive guidance. With the later development of our mental faculties we tended to disparage these senses as we became more and more enchanted with the physical world.

By relying exclusively on our physical senses and reasoning faculties, our senses of higher perception atrophied from neglect. Recognising this, New Age people are taking measures to achieve a balance between the sensory and rational faculties. Strong forces are leading us to restore equilibrium because of our innate yearning for paradise.

Intuition and ESP are regarded as metaphysical senses as they both function at higher frequency levels and are of a much finer nature than the five physical senses. They require more alertness and finer attunement. Intuition is really our sixth sense because, to a greater or lesser degree, it is common to everyone. ESP should be regarded as the seventh sense, for it comes with greater sensitivity and awareness. As we engage in regular practice with numerology, our precognitive senses of intuition and ESP are being subtly but regularly employed. With every analysis, we grow a little more aware of the vast creative plan of life as it is expressed through each individual. Gradually, numerology becomes a means of comprehending the limitlessness of creation, exemplified through human expression and awareness.

To the intelligent person, nothing is more exhilarating than to engage in something that expands consciousness. Applied numerology is so satisfying in this regard that there is an early tendency toward over-enthusiasm. That early excitement, arising from the discovery of insights into the inner self, must be contained to avoid the errors of judgement that inevitably accompany immaturity in any field. Especially with a psychic science, we must exercise great restraint to avoid the temptation of jumping to hasty conclusions. Any early errors will, of course, rapidly teach the thinking person to be more discreet and to embrace greater diplomacy in revealing the results of our analyses. Such slips should not be regarded as mistakes or failures (either of the person or the system) ,but rather as lessons intended to develop our understanding.

The blossoming of our greater awareness brings with it a progressively more uncanny accuracy in our assessment of the person being analysed. Our metaphysical senses are now enjoying greater spontaneous use, with a noticeable sharpening of intuition and our ability to link up with the subject (extrasensory contact).

Every successful numerologist has achieved proficiency through the ability to see beyond the form of numbers – into their essence, as it were. Relying solely on the information conveyed by the actual numbers of the charts will, of itself, provide valuable guidance. But to delve beyond this information uncovers important insights not otherwise obtainable.

It is true that not everyone can develop intuitiveness and ESP to the same penetrating degree. The vital factors determining the successful unfolding of these senses are related to a person's own level of spiritual attunement. This is fundamentally determined by the amount of spiritual strength available to them as indicated by the Soul Plane of their Birth Chart, their Ruling Number and, to a lesser extent, by the spiritual factors in their name. People with two 2s on their Birth Chart have a higher chance of achieving success in the development of their psychic senses, doing so with less effort than those not so favourably endowed. However, it is very often more a matter of what you do with your talents than what you have been given.

Of this every reader may be sure: if you did not have the potential for advanced psychic awareness, you would have lost interest in the subject of numerology long before now. You would certainly not have read this far into the book.

We must always realise that our emerging psychic awareness can only blossom when our values are altruistic. If personal gain, unfair advantage, or other unworldly motives underlie our purpose in learning or applying numerology, our successes would be hampered by a unique aspect of spiritual law that seems to stand guardian over life's esoteric knowledge: the more we learn, the greater our responsibility for that knowledge. Our life, therefore, must itself be an example of truth and wisdom in action. For if our metaphysical senses are to develop to a point of reliable guidance, our emotions must always be under control, our mental processes always clear and unpolluted. Pure guidance has never been known to come through confused, cluttered or corrupt pathways.

CHAPTER .16

Reincarnation – Do we have a choice?

$\mathcal{V}$ery few concepts in life appear to polarise individual opinion as much as the question of reincarnation. On the one hand, those who accept it as a fact of life are at peace with the principles, finding them rational and workable. On the other hand, those who believe in the concept of only one human life have their religious or agnostic faith on which to rely in place of answers to so many metaphysical questions.

The first group embraces the Eastern religious systems and some of those now developing in the West. The second group is largely based on what we now call Christianity, a collection of some 1,200 religions originating with Roman Catholicism, itself a mixture of ancient Judaism and Roman Imperialism, formed some three centuries after the crucifixion of Jesus. With respect to both groups, I do not wish to argue or to detract from the scientific validity of numerology, for it does not depend on a belief for or against reincarnation. However, for those who do accept and seek to know more about reincarnation as the progressive embodiment of the soul in successive human forms, numerology can throw a strong light.

History records that Pythagoras taught reincarnation (not transmigration as some writers erroneously suggest), inculcating it in his philosophy as vital to the moral code of human behaviour. For he realised that whatever we do carries with it an eternal responsibility, one that does not disappear when the body disintegrates.

(If only modern decision-makers were so aware, this planet would not be in its current ecological mess!) Pythagoras also held respect for those who found it difficult or undesirable to accept reincarnation, saying that, in time, all would become aware of the truth, even if it meant dying first.

For those to whom reincarnation is a valid part of eternal life, it provides reasons for relationships, experiences and situations that would otherwise defy conventional logic. Everything on Earth is an aspect of cyclic change, enabling the analytical human mind to chart predictions. But we get to a point in our evolution when we have graduated and emancipated ourselves from the karmic cycle. Once we begin to realise that the two most painful things our body has to endure are death and birth, and that we spend all our adolescence and most of our maturity re-acquainting ourselves with where we terminated our growth during our last cycle, we begin to recognise the futility of adhering to the karmic cycle and commence to set ourselves free.

None of us is born perfect. Hence our purpose here is to evolve toward perfection. And when we become aware of how this can be achieved, we realise that we need to stay here a long time to fulfil such a mission, rather than waste time in successive re-acquaintances with our physical bodies and this planet's unique spectrum of vibrations. This is where we definitely have a choice – to grow a little each lifetime or to stay here and get it all done, making the very best of what we have.

Staying on the karmic wheel requires little choice – we just keep doing what we have always done. But to make the momentous decision to stay here until our growth has been completed demands enormous strength of fortitude, temperance, awareness and courage. It also demands maintaining our body in a state of optimum health so that it can continue to function as the noble messenger for the soul's evolution. All this requires expanding knowledge of our physical, mental and spiritual Selves, an awareness of which numerology can provide a vital key.

This will mean a whole new approach to life and living. Are you ready for the exciting experiences that will now accompany life?

I look forward to sharing the journey with you, but remember as we travel, is not the way the wind is blowing that determines our progress – over that we have no control; progress is only achieved by the way we set our sails.

We hope you enjoyed reading this Hay House Book.
If you would like to receive a free catalogue
featuring additional Hay House books and
products, or if you would like information about
the Hay Foundation, please contact:

Hay House, Inc.
P.O. Box 5100
Carlsbad, CA 92018-5100
www.hayhouse.com

***

Published and distributed in Australia by:
Hay House Australia Pty. Ltd. • 18/36 Ralph St.
Alexandria NSW 2015 • Phone: 612-9669-4299
Fax: 612-9669-4144 • www.hayhouse.com.au

Published and distributed in the United Kingdom by:
Hay House UK, Ltd. • Unit 62, Canalot Studios
222 Kensal Rd., London W10 5BN • Phone: 44-20-8962-1230
Fax: 44-20-8962-1239 • www.hayhouse.co.uk

Published and distributed in the Republic of South Africa by:
Hay House SA (Pty), Ltd., P.O. Box 990, Witkoppen 2068
Phone/Fax: 2711-7012233 • orders@psdprom.co.za

Distributed in Canada by: Raincoast,
9050 Shaughnessy St., Vancouver, B.C. V6P 6E5
Phone: (604) 323-7100 • Fax: (604) 323-2600